THE
POWHATAN
TRIBES

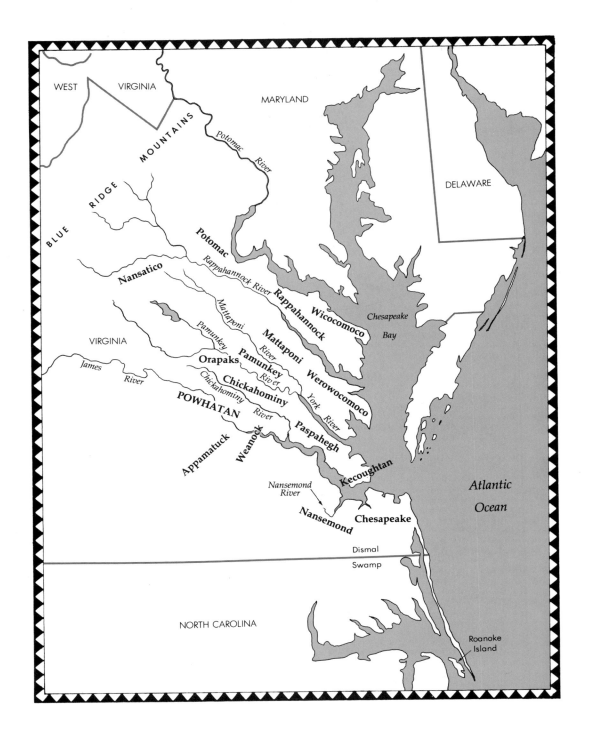

THE POWHATAN TRIBES

Christian F. Feest
Museum für Völkerkunde, Vienna, Austria

Frank W. Porter III
General Editor

C H E L S E A   H O U S E   P U B L I S H E R S
New York   Philadelphia

On the cover Skin garment decorated with shells, known as "Powhatan's mantle," made in the early 1600s.

Chelsea House Publishers
Editor-in-Chief Nancy Toff
Executive Editor Remmel T. Nunn
Managing Editor Karyn Gullen Browne
Copy Chief Juliann Barbato
Picture Editor Adrian G. Allen
Art Director Maria Epes
Manufacturing Manager Gerald Levine

Indians of North America
Senior Editor Liz Sonneborn

Staff for **THE POWHATAN TRIBES**
Associate Editor Clifford W. Crouch
Deputy Copy Chief Nicole Bowen
Assistant Art Director Loraine Machlin
Designer Donna Sinisgalli
Design Assistant James Baker
Picture Researcher Robert Shamis
Production Manager Joseph Romano
Production Coordinator Marie Claire Cebrián

7 9 8 6

Library of Congress Cataloging-in-Publication Data

Feest, Christian F.
   The Powhatan tribes / Christian F. Feest.
      p.   cm.—(Indians of North America)
   Bibliography: p.
   Includes index.
   Summary: Examines the history, culture, and changing fortunes of the Powhatan Indians.
   ISBN 1-55546-726-1
         0-7910-0395-7 (pbk.)
   1. Powhatan Indians.   [1. Powhatan Indians.   2. Indians of North America.] I. Title. II. Series: Indians of North America (Chelsea House Publishers)
                                                     89-9975
E99.P85F44   1989   CIP
973'.04973—dc20   AC

CONTENTS

INDIANS OF NORTH AMERICA

CHELSEA HOUSE PUBLISHERS

INDIANS OF NORTH AMERICA: CONFLICT AND SURVIVAL

Frank W. Porter III

The Indians survived our open intention of wiping them out, and since the tide turned they have even weathered our good intentions toward them, which can be much more deadly.

John Steinbeck
America and Americans

When Europeans first reached the North American continent, they found hundreds of tribes occupying a vast and rich country. The newcomers quickly recognized the wealth of natural resources. They were not, however, so quick or willing to recognize the spiritual, cultural, and intellectual riches of the people they called Indians.

The Indians of North America examines the problems that develop when people with different cultures come together. For American Indians, the consequences of their interaction with non-Indian people have been both productive and tragic. The Europeans believed they had "discovered" a "New World," but their religious bigotry, cultural bias, and materialistic world view kept them from appreciating and understanding the people who lived in it. All too often they attempted to change the way of life of the indigenous people. The Spanish conquistadores wanted the Indians as a source of labor. The Christian missionaries, many of whom were English, viewed them as potential converts. French traders and trappers used the Indians as a means to obtain pelts. As Francis Parkman, the 19th-century historian, stated, "Spanish civilization crushed the Indian; English civilization scorned and neglected him; French civilization embraced and cherished him."

7

Nearly 500 years later, many people think of American Indians as curious vestiges of a distant past, waging a futile war to survive in a Space Age society. Even today, our understanding of the history and culture of American Indians is too often derived from unsympathetic, culturally biased, and inaccurate reports. The American Indian, described and portrayed in thousands of movies, television programs, books, articles, and government studies, has either been raised to the status of the "noble savage" or disparaged as the "wild Indian" who resisted the westward expansion of the American frontier.

Where in this popular view are the real Indians, the human beings and communities whose ancestors can be traced back to ice-age hunters? Where are the creative and indomitable people whose sophisticated technologies used the natural resources to ensure their survival, whose military skill might even have prevented European settlement of North America if not for devastating epidemics and disruption of the ecology? Where are the men and women who are today diligently struggling to assert their legal rights and express once again the value of their heritage?

The various Indian tribes of North America, like people everywhere, have a history that includes population expansion, adaptation to a range of regional environments, trade across wide networks, internal strife, and warfare. This was the reality. Europeans justified their conquests, however, by creating a mythical image of the New World and its native people. In this myth, the New World was a virgin land, waiting for the Europeans. The arrival of Christopher Columbus ended a timeless primitiveness for the original inhabitants.

Also part of this myth was the debate over the origins of the American Indians. Fantastic and diverse answers were proposed by the early explorers, missionairies, and settlers. Some thought that the Indians were descended from the Ten Lost Tribes of Israel, others that they were descended from inhabitants of the lost continent of Atlantis. One writer suggested that the Indians had reached North America in another Noah's ark.

A later myth, perpetrated by many historians, focused on the relentless persecution during the past five centuries until only a scattering of these "primitive" people remained to be herded onto reservations. This view fails to chronicle the overt and covert ways in which the Indians successfully coped with the intruders.

All of these myths presented one-sided interpretations that ignored the complexity of European and American events and policies. All left serious questions unanswered. What were the origins of the American Indians? Where did they come from? How and when did they get to the New World? What was their life—their culture—really like?

In the late 1800s, anthropologists and archaeologists in the Smithsonian Institution's newly created Bureau of American Ethnology in Washington,

D.C., began to study scientifically the history and culture of the Indians of North America. They were motivated by an honest belief that the Indians were on the verge of extinction and that along with them would vanish their languages, religious beliefs, technology, myths, and legends. These men and women went out to visit, study, and record data from as many Indian communities as possible before this information was forever lost.

By this time there was a new myth in the national consciousness. American Indians existed as figures in the American past. They had performed a historical mission. They had challenged white settlers who trekked across the continent. Once conquered, however, they were supposed to accept graciously the way of life of their conquerors.

The reality again was different. American Indians resisted both actively and passively. They refused to lose their unique identity, to be assimilated into white society. Many whites viewed the Indians not only as members of a conquered nation but also as "inferior" and "unequal." The rights of the Indians could be expanded, contracted, or modified as the conquerors saw fit. In every generation, white society asked itself what to do with the American Indians. Their answers have resulted in the twists and turns of federal Indian policy.

There were two general approaches. One way was to raise the Indians to a "higher level" by "civilizing" them. Zealous missionaries considered it their Christian duty to elevate the Indian through conversion and scanty education. The other approach was to ignore the Indians until they disappeared under pressure from the ever-expanding white society. The myth of the "vanishing Indian" gave stronger support to the latter option, helping to justify the taking of the Indians' land.

Prior to the end of the 18th century, there was no national policy on Indians simply because the American nation has not yet come into existence. American Indians similarly did not possess a political or social unity with which to confront the various Europeans. They were not homogeneous. Rather, they were loosely formed bands and tribes, speaking nearly 300 languages and thousands of dialects. The collective identity felt by Indians today is a result of their common experiences of defeat and/or mistreatment at the hands of whites.

During the colonial period, the British crown did not have a coordinated policy toward the Indians of North America. Specific tribes (most notably the Iroquois and the Cherokee) became military and political pawns used by both the crown and the individual colonies. The success of the American Revolution brought no immediate change. When the United States acquired new territory from France and Mexico in the early 19th century, the federal government wanted to open this land to settlement by homesteaders. But the Indian tribes that lived on this land had signed treaties with European governments assuring their title to the land. Now the United States assumed legal responsibility for honoring these treaties.

At first, President Thomas Jefferson believed that the Louisiana Purchase contained sufficient land for both the Indians and the white population. Within a generation, though, it became clear that the Indians would not be allowed to remain. In the 1830s the federal government began to coerce the eastern tribes to sign treaties agreeing to relinquish their ancestral land and move west of the Mississippi River. Whenever these negotiations failed, President Andrew Jackson used the military to remove the Indians. The southeastern tribes, promised food and transportation during their removal to the West, were instead forced to walk the "Trail of Tears." More than 4,000 men, woman, and children died during this forced march. The "removal policy" was successful in opening the land to homesteaders, but it created enormous hardships for the Indians.

By 1871 most of the tribes in the United States had signed treaties ceding most or all of their ancestral land in exchange for reservations and welfare. The treaty terms were intended to bind both parties for all time. But in the General Allotment Act of 1887, the federal government changed its policy again. Now the goal was to make tribal members into individual landowners and farmers, encouraging their absorption into white society. This policy was advantageous to whites who were eager to acquire Indian land, but it proved disastrous for the Indians. One hundred thirty-eight million acres of reservation land were subdivided into tracts of 160, 80, or as little as 40 acres, and allotted tribe members on an individual basis. Land owned in this way was said to have "trust status" and could not be sold. But the surplus land—all Indian land not allotted to individuals—was opened (for sale) to white settlers. Ultimately, more than 90 million acres of land were taken from the Indians by legal and illegal means.

The resulting loss of land was a catastrophe for the Indians. It was necessary to make it illegal for Indians to sell their land to non-Indians. The Indian Reorganization Act of 1934 officially ended the allotment period. Tribes that voted to accept the provisions of this act were reorganized, and an effort was made to purchase land within preexisting reservations to restore an adequate land base.

Ten years later, in 1944, federal Indian policy again shifted. Now the federal government wanted to get out of the "Indian business." In 1953 an act of Congress named specific tribes whose trust status was to be ended "at the earliest possible time." This new law enabled the United States to end unilaterally, whether the Indians wished it or not, the special status that protected the land in Indian tribal reservations. In the 1950s federal Indian policy was to transfer federal responsibility and jurisdiction to state governments, encourage the physical relocation of Indian peoples from reservations to urban areas, and hasten the termination, or extinction, of tribes.

Between 1954 and 1962 Congress passed specific laws authorizing the termination of more than 100 tribal groups. The stated purpose of the termination policy was to ensure the full and complete integration of Indians into American society. However, there is a less benign way to interpret this legislation. Even as termination was being discussed in Congress, 133 separate bills were introduced to permit the transfer of trust land ownership from Indians to non-Indians.

With the Johnson administration in the 1960s the federal government began to reject termination. In the 1970s yet another Indian policy emerged. Known as "self-determination," it favored keeping the protective role of the federal government while increasing tribal participation in, and control of, important areas of local government. In 1983 President Reagan, in a policy statement on Indian affairs, restated the unique "government is government" relationship of the United States with the Indians. However, federal programs since then have moved toward transferring Indian affairs to individual states, which have long desired to gain control of Indian land and resources.

As long as American Indians retain power, land, and resources that are coveted by the states and the federal government, there will continue to be a "clash of cultures," and the issues will be contested in the courts, Congress, the White House, and even in the international human rights community. To give all Americans a greater comprehension of the issues and conflicts involving American Indians today is a major goal of this series. These issues are not easily understood, nor can these conflicts be readily resolved. The study of North American Indian history and culture is a necessary and important step toward that comprehension. All Americans must learn the history of the relations between the Indians and the federal government, recognize the unique legal status of the Indians, and understand the heritage and cultures of the Indians of North America.

A romanticized 19th-century illustration of Pocahontas's rescue of John Smith—an incident the English captain may have fabricated. Whether or not Powhatan's daughter did in fact save Smith from execution by her tribesmen in 1608, she was about 10 years old at the time, far younger than she appears here.

BEFORE
JAMESTOWN

A father and daughter are the best-known figures in the history of the Indian tribes known as the Powhatan. He gave his people their name; she became a legendary character in the history of colonial America. The two have come to symbolize power and mercy, tenacity and compromise, autonomy and conciliation, fact and fable. The father was the Indian chief Powhatan, and his daughter the celebrated Pocahontas.

The legend of Pocahontas begins with the colonization of eastern North America by the British at the start of the 17th century, at a settlement called Jamestown in what is now the state of Virginia. According to the writings of Captain John Smith, one of the settlement's founders, Indians captured Smith while he and his men were exploring the surrounding territory.

Smith's captors took him to their village, forced him to kneel on a stone altar, and prepared to crush his skull with their heavy war clubs. At that moment a young girl named Pocahontas, the favorite daughter of the tribe's chief, threw herself over the captain's body. Thus shielding him, she pleaded for his life. After he was spared, Pocahontas further interceded on behalf of the colonists, who were starving after a poor harvest. By persuading her people to bring food to the residents of Jamestown, she in effect rescued all of them as well—and thereby, just possibly, the future United States of America.

The tale of Pocahontas is well known but probably untrue. The real story of her people, who played an important role in the early British settlement of America and who have survived almost four centuries of domination by the descendants of those colonists, has been told much less often.

The approximately 30 Indian groups now known as the Powhatan tribes were originally joined only by 2 factors: their languages, which were a part of a family of related languages called Algonquian, and the location of their homelands on an inlet of the Middle Atlantic coast now called Chesapeake Bay in present-day Virginia and Maryland. At about the end of the 1500s— just before the arrival of British settlers—these peoples were forcibly united into a political confederacy by Powhatan, who by birthright was chief of several of the tribes. But this unity was shattered within a few decades of his death. Thus, strictly speaking, there were no Powhatan tribes before about 1570 or after 1650, but only various Algonquian-speaking tribes (also called Algonkians) living in what is now Virginia.

About 3,000 years ago, Algonkians inhabited the region north of the Great Lakes, fishing and hunting moose to survive. From there they spread west, east, and south. Those in the west learned to hunt the bison that roamed the prairies of the Great Plains; those in the temperate woodlands south of the Great Lakes and east of the Appalachian Mountains began to grow corn amid the forest clearings.

By the end of the 15th century, when Europeans first came to North America, the Algonkians had spread across the continent over an area roughly resembling a triangle. This triangle extended from the Rocky Mountains of present-day Alberta, Canada, in the northwest, to the Labrador Peninsula in eastern Canada, and down to Cape Lookout in present-day North Carolina in the south. The Algonkians shared this vast expanse with only the Iroquoian-speaking peoples living along what are now the eastern Great Lakes and with a few scattered tribes of the Sioux language family.

Within what is now Virginia, the Algonkians inhabited only the coastal lowlands along Chesapeake Bay and the Atlantic Ocean. The western boundary of their territory was marked by the sudden drop-off in land elevation from a vast plateau area called the Piedmont. At this abrupt slope, the area's rivers came rushing down, propelled onward by the drop in altitude from the adjoining Blue Ridge Mountains, part of the immense Appalachian mountain chain.

Once the rivers have reached the coastal lowlands, their flow is affected by the tides of the Atlantic, and for a considerable distance inland from Chesapeake Bay the water is brackish— a mixture of salty ocean and fresh river water. For this reason, the region has become known as the Tidewater area of Virginia.

Chesapeake Bay itself is the bed of an old river that over centuries became submerged into the Atlantic. Now fed by many rivers, the bay divides the mainland on the west from the Delmarva Peninsula—so named after the states *Delaware, Maryland* and *Virginia*. (The peninsula is also known locally as the Eastern Shore.) Along the bay's southwestern shore, four major rivers further divide the Tidewater area into three other peninsulas: the Northern Neck, which is south of the Potomac River and north of the Rappahannock; the Middle Peninsula, which is south of the Rappahannock River and north of the York; and the Virginia Peninsula, which is south of the York River and north of the James. The mainland area south of the James River is known as Southside Virginia. To the south of this lies the Dismal Swamp, one of many swamps on the coastal plain that separated the Tidewater Algonkians from related tribes living in what is now North Carolina.

In the heart of the Powhatan tribes' traditional territory, the York River

A photograph taken by anthropologist Frank Speck in 1920 of the falls of the Rappahannock River, near a prehistoric Indian village outside Fredericksburg, Virginia. Many Powhatan tribes depended on the Tidewater region's network of rivers and saltwater inlets for fish, oysters, and mussels.

A Spanish map of eastern North America and South America, drawn in the late 1500s. Spaniards made contact with the Powhatan decades before the English founded the settlement of Jamestown in their territory.

splits into the Pamunkey and Mattaponi rivers, and the James River divides into the Chickahominy and James rivers. All of these rivers were literally lifelines for the people dwelling along their banks. Not only did they allow for communication and trade by boat, they provided enormous quantities of fish. The bay itself was a vast bed of mussels and oysters. Birds, especially waterfowl, attracted by the streams became easy prey for hunters.

The warm and humid climate supported the natural growth of mixed oak and pine forests north of the James River and pine forests to the south. It also enabled the people to grow corn and other crops in gardens close to the riverbanks. When occasional severe droughts ruined these gardens, the tribes could still obtain food by fishing, hunting, and gathering wild roots and berries. Hunters regularly shot or trapped animals such as raccoons, foxes, beavers, otters, muskrats, hares, and opossums. Deer and bears could also be found in the Tidewater area, but they were most common in the higher elevations, which were both far from the good fishing grounds and close to enemy territory. Consequently, the Powhatan hunted these animals mostly during winter, when the tribes had gathered together for the season.

Humans had occupied the Tidewater area of Virginia for thousands of years, long before the coming of the Algonkians. Exactly when the ancestors of the Powhatan tribes made their appearance is a matter of speculation. It is likely that various groups drifted into coastal Virginia separately and over a long period. This migration was certainly southward along the Atlantic coast, for we know that the Powhatan tribes had other Algonquian-speaking neighbors in this area. To their west and south, however, lived Siouan and Iroquoian tribes, traditional enemies of the coastal Algonquian-speaking peoples.

The Piedmont was inhabited by speakers of Siouan languages, such as the Tutelo, Saponi, and Occaneechi, who were relatives of the Dakota and other western tribes. In Southside Virginia, south of the Blackwater River, lived the Iroquoian-speaking Nottoway and Meherrin, and, still farther south, the Tuscarora. Little is known today about the relations of the Powhatan people to these tribes, save that they engaged in sporadic warfare, broken by occasional alliances.

Only a generation after Christopher Columbus first crossed the Atlantic in 1492 to explore the Caribbean, and John Cabot followed in 1497 and claimed Newfoundland, the first Europeans made their appearance in Chesapeake Bay. Although the area has long been associated with the British settlers of Jamestown, its first visitors were in fact Spanish and Portuguese explorers, raiding the Atlantic coast for Indian slaves and searching for a shortcut to China. Spanish maps of the 1520s reflect a fairly detailed knowledge of the region. These explorers established no settlements but probably conducted some trade with the Indians they met. European ships wrecked on the Outer Banks near Cape Hatteras became the first source of iron for the Indians. This metal probably soon reached the Indians of Virginia through trade routes.

Sometime around the year 1560, Spain decided to attempt to establish a colony in the area. As part of this design, a Spanish expedition kidnapped a young Indian, who they subsequently discovered was the offspring of a tribal chief of the Tidewater area. He was taken to Havana, Cuba—the center of Spanish colonial operations—where he was instructed in Spanish manners and Christianity. He was baptized and given the name of his godfather, Don Luis de Velasco, who was the viceroy (supreme ruler) of New Spain. The newly renamed Don Luis offered to escort a group of missionaries to his home country, which he called Ajacan, but a first attempt to reach Chesapeake Bay failed in 1566. The Indian Don Luis was subsequently taken to Spain, where he was introduced to King Philip II.

In 1570, Don Luis finally returned to present-day Virginia, accompanied by Father Juan Bautista de Segura and a few other missionaries who were members of the Society of Jesus, also called the Jesuits. Don Luis found his people starving after a prolonged drought and immediately deserted the missionaries, who nonetheless proceeded to found a mission on the banks of the nearby York River. They attempted to convert the Indians there to Christianity and in the process introduced to them previously unknown items such as metal utensils and spun cloth. The Indians were initially friendly toward and interested in their visitors but soon withdrew from the vicinity of the mission. Although he rejoined his tribe, Don Luis refused to accept the chieftainship he had inherited, at least for the time being. Early in 1571, he returned to visit the mission with a war party and killed the Jesuits— apparently a supreme display of his ut-

The slaying of Father Juan Bautista de Segura and fellow Jesuit missionaries by Tidewater warriors in 1571. This illustration was published in a 17th-century study of the Jesuits by Mathias Tanner.

ter rejection of Spanish culture. Only one Spaniard, an altar boy named Alonso, escaped. He found refuge among a group of Indians, perhaps in the village of Kecoughtan, at the mouth of the James River.

Later that year, the crew of a Spanish supply ship found the mission deserted and the Indians wearing the Jesuits' priestly garments. In retaliation, Spain mounted an expedition the following year that retrieved Alonso and killed more than 30 Indians. The first extended encounter between Eu-

ropeans and the tribes of the Tidewater area had not been a happy one, and for more than a decade afterward, there were few European expeditions to the vicinity.

In 1584, a party of Englishmen explored the area in hopes of establishing a settlement. They were met with hostility by the people of Southside Virginia. Nonetheless, two shiploads of colonists attempted an encampment on Roanoke Island, off the coast of present-day North Carolina. This effort failed, but renewed contact with natives seemed much friendlier.

In 1587, a second attempt to build a colony was undertaken at this location. Under the authorization of Sir Walter Raleigh, 3 ships carrying 117 people, including women and children, landed on the island. When the colony, which was named Roanoke, began to run low on supplies, its leader, John White, set sail for England. Upon his return in 1590, Roanoke Colony had vanished. The mystery of its fate has never been solved, and to this day Roanoke is commonly known as the Lost Colony. Subsequent British colonists recorded rumors that the inhabitants of the settlement had been massacred by members of the Powhatan tribes.

Spanish ships entered Chesapeake Bay in 1588 in an unsuccessful search for a competing British settlement. Their contacts with the Indians were mostly peaceful, but they shanghaied two tribesmen for use as guides and interpreters. There is little doubt that such contacts became increasingly common, especially as the British prepared themselves for another attempt at colonizing North America.

In April 1606, King James I of Great Britain granted a charter for the establishment of the colony of Virginia, which was to be financed by a company of London merchants. In December of that year the flagship *Susan Constant*, accompanied by the *Godspeed* and a smaller vessel named the *Discovery*, carried more aspiring settlers from London to Chesapeake Bay. Delayed by adverse winds and layovers in the Caribbean for new provisions, they did not enter the bay until 18 weeks later. The colonists promptly erected a cross at the bay's mouth, then proceeded westward, up the James River. Their arrival and subsequent establishment of Jamestown, which became the first permanent English settlement in America, would forever change the world of the Powhatan people. ▲

Modern reconstructions of the Susan Constant, Discovery, *and* Godspeed, *the three ships of the first Virginia colonists.*

A page from Thomas Hariot's Brief and True Report of the New Found Land of Virginia, *published in 1590. The engraving, by Theodore de Bry, shows Tidewater Indians making a dugout canoe. Hariot notes that the laborers first burn a cavity into the log, then "that which they think is sufficiently burned they quench and scrape away with shells."*

PEOPLE
OF THE
TIDEWATER

The first night of our landing, about midnight, there came some Savages sayling close to our quarter," wrote Sir George Percy, a member of the 1607 British expedition that founded the colony of Virginia. "Presently there was an alarum given; upon that, the Savages ran away, and we [were] not troubled any more by them that night." The Powhatan people, understandably cautious, were careful to avoid British scrutiny—perhaps to give themselves time in which to assess the newcomers' intentions.

On April 27, 1607, a small advance party of Englishmen undertook an exploratory trek into the wilderness. "We could not see a Savage in all that march," Percy noted in his diary. In a few days, however, the party spotted "five Savages running on the shoare." The English greeted these men with what they called "a signe of friendship"—placing a hand over their heart—and in return were cordially invited to the Indian village of Kecoughtan. There the people entertained the colonists with a feast and dancing.

Kecoughtan was very much a typical Indian settlement of the area, though such villages varied considerably in size. About 20 houses stood in scattered groups, separated by little groves of trees. The arched roofs of the houses reminded the English of the arbors in their gardens back home. The dwellings' tunnel-shaped frames were formed from bent saplings with their ends implanted in the ground and poles that were lashed across the saplings horizontally. Covering these poles, to form the walls and the roof, were mats woven from rushes (a marsh plant) or broad strips of bark peeled from trees.

Each single-room house had two entrances, one at each end of the narrow building. Some of the rush mats could be rolled up to let in additional daylight and fresh air. Fires for cooking and heat in the winter were lit inside the dwellings. The smoke rising from these indoor fires escaped through gaps between the mats or through small holes left in the roof. Along the interior walls sat low platforms—made of wooden posts and beams—covered with mats. These platforms served as beds, on which people slept with their heads pointing toward the fire at the center of the room.

In the spring, most of the women and some elderly men worked in gardens surrounding the village. Between April and June, they planted corn, beans, squash, gourds, and passionflowers (which produce edible berries) on land that the men had first cleared of undergrowth. After loosening the soil with simple hoes, the women poked holes in the earth about every three feet using pointed sticks. Into each hole they dropped three to five kernels of corn and a few beans and then covered them with small mounds of dirt. Other vegetables were planted in the space between these mounds.

The Indians grew one plant in its own distinct patch: a local variety of tobacco. This plant was native to the Americas, but Europeans would soon embrace it avidly. Later colonial farmers would raise a variety native to Brazil, and within a few years English tobacco would become a drug used worldwide and thus a crop of major monetary importance.

Older Powhatan children helped their mothers plant and weed the gardens. After planting, and throughout the spring and summer, the children and older people safeguarded the seeds and young plants by shouting and throwing stones at scavenging birds and animals.

While the women were tending the gardens, most men either fished or stalked the woods alone for deer, squirrels, beavers, rabbits, raccoons, opossums, and wild turkeys. Each man hunted with a wooden bow, fitted with a string made of either animal gut or a strip of twisted deerskin, from which he shot wooden arrows tipped with triangular points of stone. In areas such as Kecoughtan, where there were no rocks that could be used to make arrowheads, men instead fashioned the tips out of bones, antlers, bird beaks, or turkey spurs—the short, stiff spines that protrude from the bird's claws. Men tried to better their deer-hunting prospects by camouflaging themselves in deerskins. They also caught small game in snares, which trapped any unsuspecting animals that blundered into concealed nooses attached to bent-sapling triggers.

The men from villages near rivers and inlets gave first priority to catching fish and collecting oysters and mussels, either by wading in shallow water or fishing from wooden dugout canoes up to 50 feet long. They fished with nets made of twisted animal sinew, bark, or plant fibers; with fishing rods and lines baited on bone hooks; with many-pronged spears; and even with their bows, from which they shot arrows tied to long cords. Sometimes they barricaded waterways with dams of stone or fences of wooden stakes to trap fish so that they could be caught more easily. Now and then men also fished at night, attracting their prey with the light from fires that they set inside their boats.

In the summer, women, old men, and children gathered roots and berries to supplement the diet. Some corn was eaten in July, when it was still green, but the main harvest began in August and lasted until October. Because food was plentiful in late summer and early

A modern reconstruction of a Tidewater Indian dwelling. This replica, located in Jamestown Settlement, Virginia, is part of a historically authentic model of a colonial-era settlement.

A 16th-century engraving by Theodore de Bry of the Powhatan's method of drying fish. Food preserved this way was stored and eaten in the winter.

autumn, this time of year was devoted to feasting and to the tribe's most important religious ceremonies. Virtually nothing is known of these ceremonies, however, as the arriving English colonists took little note of Powhatan religious observances.

In autumn, walnuts, hickory nuts, acorns, and chestnuts were ready for gathering by the women, children, and older men. Some of these foods, along with a portion of the corn crop, were stored for winter eating in underground pits in the woods and on mat-covered scaffolds next to the houses. People also preserved some meat, fish, and oysters by drying them over fires.

After the trees had shed their leaves and the wild geese and other birds had returned from their summer haunts in the north, it was time for the tribes' annual winter hunts. Everyone but the very young, very old, and very feeble then moved to winter hunting camps, which were located where the land began to rise into the Piedmont and more mountainous areas. Women rolled up the canopylike mats of their houses and carried them, along with other important household belongings, in packs on their back. At each camp, people set up small shelters by placing the housing mats over simple wooden frames.

Usually several villages joined together in the hunting season, and 200 or more hunters might commonly band together. These bands surrounded herds of deer, flushing them from the underbrush with fire, shouts, and the aid of tame dogs. Sometimes they drove the deer into nearby lakes or rivers, where they were easily killed by hunters waiting in boats. The Indians hunted and fished in these large groups until early spring—perhaps around March—when they returned to their home village.

Hunting provided all the tribes' meat, for they raised no domestic animals, except for dogs and perhaps some tame birds. Aside from meat, hunting gave the Indians a number of raw materials. Most of the Tidewater people's clothing was made of animal skins, and they fashioned tools from bones and antlers. The hair of deer, the claws of pumas (mountain lions), and the skins of snakes were used to make ornaments, which were worn by both men and women.

The type of ornaments a person wore depended upon his or her wealth. Shell beads, for example, were generally obtained by trade from tribes such as the Nanticoke along the upper reaches of Chesapeake Bay. Objects made of these beads were also used as money. When visiting other tribes, representatives of the Tidewater people gave authority to their words by offering gifts of shell beads strung into headbands or necklaces.

Copper beads were likewise luxury items received in trade from far away, perhaps from the Indians of the Great Lakes region, and were worn exclusively by the rich. Headbands of copper and hair ornaments made of red-dyed deer hair served as even clearer distinctions of rank and could only be worn by certain chiefs. Bonnets made of feathers (possibly eagle or turkey) also denoted their authority.

Like ornaments, hairstyle and dress were signs of people's role and status in their village and tribe. Male adults used a sharp reed or piece of shell to shave the right side of their head in order to prevent their hair from becoming entangled with the drawstring of their bow during hunting or warfare. They let the hair on the left side grow into a long cascade, which they greased with walnut oil and often tied into a knot and adorned with feathers. Priests were known by a small lock grown on the shaven right side of their head. Married women wore their hair cropped in one length, just below their ears. Unmarried women, however, cut their hair close to their forehead and temples but let it grow long in the back.

Women also tattooed figures of animals and plants on their face and body, an effect that they achieved by rubbing soot into incisions slit in their skin with copper knives. Men did not have tattoos but did paint themselves, using different colors and designs according to the occasion. For this they used dyes obtained from minerals and plants.

Dress differed less between women and men than between rich and poor. The least wealthy people covered themselves with little but leaves and long grasses woven together and tucked into broad leather belts. Both sexes commonly wore these breechcloths like aprons. They reached almost to the wearers' knees but left their backside exposed. Deerskin leggings and moccasins were worn for protection in winter, on hunting trips, and on war expeditions. The wealthy wore robes made of finely prepared leather embroidered with shell or copper beads, or they wove cloaks made of raccoon skin or turkey feathers that had been intricately woven into a warm and shining fabric. Priests also wore mantles made of these materials, but theirs were distinguished by their peculiar cut.

Extended families of from 6 to 20 members commonly shared a house. Such households often included a married couple, their children, and the parents of either the wife or husband. Sometimes the families of brothers shared a house. And in some cases, a man might marry more than one woman and thus raise more than one family. Only a rich man could do so, however, for every man was expected to give a number of valued goods, as a bride price, to the family of his intended wife. Only a good hunter could support a large household, and men were expected to support any wives they took. But in the end, the work of several wives and many children sometimes actually increased a man's wealth.

New parents always gave a feast shortly after a child's birth, inviting relatives and possibly family friends as well. At this gathering, the father announced the name of the new family member. As children grew older, they received a nickname from their mother, and that became the name by which they were commonly known.

Boys were trained early in life to become good hunters. Every morning they had to practice shooting arrows at moving targets, such as little sticks or pieces of moss that had been tossed in the air, and did not get breakfast until they had hit their mark. If a boy demonstrated some special ability or talent—perhaps in hunting or tracking—his father gave him yet another name. Likewise, if a man became known for some valorous deed in warfare, his chief would also confer a name-title on him. This name-title, which could be bestowed only by the chief, served as a special mark of honor which singled out the bearer from his peers.

Young men and women courted each other with gifts of food. The man might present wild game that he himself caught, whereas the woman would give some of the produce of her garden. As a rule, parents negotiated the bride price; some, especially members of the upper class, even decided on the proper mate for their offspring.

Each household was expected to take care of its own needs. Men hunted and fished to supply their families with meat and animal skins. They also made tools from stones and shells. With these tools they carved bowls and ladles, hollowed out logs to create canoes, and made weapons. Before Europeans introduced iron to the Indians, their arms included bows and arrows, shields made of bark, and wooden clubs with heavy ball-shaped heads.

In addition to tending the gardens and gathering wild foodstuffs, women prepared all meals. They also tanned the animal skins men provided and used bone awls and needles to make the tanned skins into clothing, leather bags, and pouches. From plant fibers, such as hemp and reeds, women wove baskets to hold food. They made pots by coiling rolls of clay that had been mixed with crushed shell or bits of quartz. After pots made from this mixture were baked in a fire, they were durable enough for use in cooking. Women also held responsibility for tending the fire, which they kindled by using a simple friction drill and tinder of dry leaves or moss.

The Powhatan people most often made music and danced for religious purposes, but these artistic activities also served as entertainment. Indeed, the people of the Tidewater pictured their happy life after death as consisting of continuous singing and dancing. The rhythms to which they sang and danced came from rattles made of dried gourds filled with pebbles or seeds, folded pieces of deerskin beaten with the player's hand, and drums made of animal skins stretched over wooden bowls. Powhatan men also played melodies on flutes they made from cane.

The tribes' sports included a hockeylike game played by men and a game similar to soccer that was probably played by the women and children together. In both games, players tried to shoot a ball into a goal marked by posts or trees. Men competed individually in footraces, boxing, and wrestling. Men also passionately played a gambling

A werowance *dressed in a breechcloth, in a 1585 watercolor by John White. Wealthy tribe members also wore cloaks of raccoon skin, turkey feathers, or ornamented leather.*

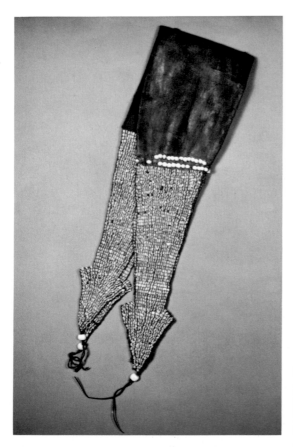

A leather bag, decorated with shell beads, made by Powhatan Indians in the early 1600s. This object, which is now in Britain's Ashmolean Museum, is one of the few Powhatan artifacts surviving from this period.

game using 81 straws. Players sometimes spent days and nights on end trying to guess the number of straws their opponent held and bet enormous sums on the outcome. An unfortunate gambler might even wager his own person and end up the winner's slave.

When a person died, the corpse was wrapped in rush mats or animal skins and then buried. Women were designated as mourners. They blackened their faces with coal and wept for a day after the death occurred. A few beads or other possessions were placed in the grave to be used by the departed in the land of the dead. The deceased's property commonly went to a male heir. In what is now northern Virginia, however, in distinction to the practices of most Powhatan tribes, bodies were laid on high platforms and allowed to decompose. Every three or four years, the bones of all those who had died during that period were interred together in huge pits.

Every village and tribe (which might consist of one or more villages) was ruled by a greatly respected leader called its *werowance* (if a man) or, less commonly, a *weronsqua* (if a woman). This position was hereditary, passing from brother to sister and then to the sister's son or daughter, as a means of transition known as *matrilineal succession*. A werowance filled the roles of both religious and governmental leader of his tribe. Collectively, the families of werowances formed a class of nobility among the people of the Tidewater, whose members selected their marriage partners from among themselves. These nobles held the bulk of the tribes' wealth and power. They dressed more elaborately and lived in bigger houses than the common people. Werowances themselves were even interred in unique fashion: Their bones were removed and cleaned, then resewn into their preserved skins and installed in the western part of the village temple. And—at least according to the werowances themselves—only they and their priests were supposed, after death, to go over the mountains in the west, to be one with the gods.

A werowance held life-and-death power over his subjects. He could order the execution of anyone he judged guilty of treason or murder and sentence people accused of minor offenses to be beaten with a club—sentences probably carried out by his personal bodyguard. The werowance was assisted in meting out punishments by the tribal priests, called the *quiyough-cosuck* (pronounced kwee-YOU-ah-suck), who were believed to possess a magical ability to identify the perpetrator of a crime. The quiyoughcosuck,

Virginia Indians performing a ceremonial dance, depicted in a 1586 watercolor by John White. Some dancers carry rattles made of gourds filled with seeds or pebbles, and others hold plant sprigs.

who might number up to half a dozen in a larger village, served as close advisors to their werowance on other matters as well. These men derived their name from a class of minor benevolent gods; these divinities were in turn counterbalanced by malignant beings called *tagkanysough*.

An elevated platform, inside a village temple, on which the preserved corpses of werowances are placed. This John White painting, which dates from 1586, also shows an image of Okewas (along wall at right) positioned so as to watch over the bodies.

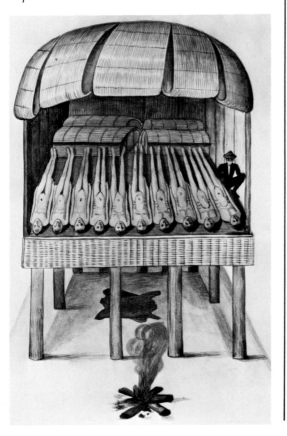

The principal god venerated by Powhatan priests and commoners alike was Okewas, a terrible, vengeful spirit whose image was kept in the village temples and carried into battle during wars against other tribes. Okewas was believed to have established the present order of the world, although he had not created it. (Interestingly, the god who had done so was not venerated.) To Indians wandering in the woods, Okewas occasionally appeared in the shape of a handsome young man who would scratch or otherwise mutilate his beholder. Misfortunes that befell the Powhatan were sometimes considered punishments meted out by Okewas for violations of the moral laws he oversaw. In order to atone for their misdeeds and appease Okewas, both priests and commoners could make offerings of tobacco, shell beads, or copper. Offerings were made to Ahone, a peaceful god, as well. The Powhatan also believed in *manitous*, nature spirits that were also acknowledged by other Algonkians.

The quiyoughcosuck performed important rituals in the village temple and identified and cured diseases by using either magic or herbs. They were also believed to be able to make clouds rain or the sun shine according to the needs of the cornfields. Some priests were also prophets and their predictions influenced the werowance's political and military decisions.

The village temple generally stood apart from the houses of the community. Often it was situated on a hill overlooking them. Men built the temple of

A tribal priest, or quiyoughcosuck, *in a 1586 watercolor by John White. The small lock of hair on the shaven right side of the priest's head was a special mark of his position.*

the same material as their homes but between 60 and 100 feet in length and with its form aligned east-west. Priests kept a fire burning continuously in the temple's eastern section, near the entrance; in the west were kept the dried bodies of past werowances, guarded by wooden images of Okewas and other spirits.

Temples also served as treasure houses of the werowances. Here skins, corn, copper, and shell beads were kept under the protection of the gods. Some of this wealth came from tributes the werowance demanded of his subjects. Some was the yield of his fields, which were planted and harvested by his male subjects. This wealth increased through tribal trade, which the werowance regulated. The accumulated wealth supported the werowance, his family, and the priests, although they all might sometimes join in the hunting and fishing. Some of the werowance's wealth was also used to reward favored tribe members, such as accomplished warriors.

Powhatan men waged war to obtain revenge, expand tribal territory, or gain female captives, who could become second wives of the warriors. Their Siouan or Iroquoian neighbors were their most common enemy, but Powhatan tribes sometimes fought fellow Tidewater Algonkians. War was declared by a council composed of the werowance, priests, and other advisory councillors, called *cockarouses.* The personal bodyguards of a werowance also became important captains in wartime.

An appointed commander—who might be the werowance himself—led the war party, and special officers drawn from the nobility enforced strict discipline. Warriors believed combat had great religious significance, as indicated by the images of Okewas carried into the battle. Warriors cut off the scalps, sometimes the entire heads, of their killed foes, because the Powhatan believed that by taking these trophies they acquired the enemies' powers. Captured men were tortured and killed for the same reason, but children and werowances were saved; the werowances were probably spared because of their status, whereas the children were probably adopted into the tribe.

Men could improve their social standing by displaying bravery in battle, and so war became an extraordinarily important social enterprise. Men practiced war games regularly in peacetime. Most actual wars were fought in winter, when large groups of men had already united for communal hunting, or in autumn shortly after the harvest, when accumulated food supplies meant that the men were temporarily relieved of the worry of providing for their families.

Aside from social advancement through battle, a family might gain prestige through its children. Boys might be selected for a religious or political career. Sometime between the ages of 10 and 15, those chosen to become priests or councillors underwent an initiation ceremony, which was known as the Huskenaw. The boys were ceremonially abducted from their families and symbolically killed so as to be reborn as "real men." For nine months the priests kept them in isolation and instructed them in secret knowledge. They were given a medicine or drug (possibly the narcotic Jim-

son weed, named after Jamestown) that was supposed to make them forget their past lives; therefore, when they returned to their village, they would be loyal only to Okewas and their werowance. The positions of the priests and councillors were not strictly hereditary, but the children selected were usually from the upper class.

Of the nearly 40 Algonkian tribes in the Tidewater area at the time the Virginia company arrived in 1607, some had recently become part of a larger chiefdom. The forced growth of this confederacy was mostly owing to the ability of Powhatan, also known as Wahunsunacock, who was the werowance of a small tribe that lived south of the falls of the James River. Through marriages between noble families of the previous generation, Powhatan had inherited power over eight tribes. These were the nearby Arrohateck and Appamatuck; the Orapaks, on the upper Chickahominy River; and the Youghtanund, Pamunkey, Mattaponi, Werowocomoco, and Kiskiack on the York River and its tributaries—near the destroyed Spanish Jesuit mission. In the 30 or so years since Powhatan assumed rule over these tribes, he had conquered approximately another 20 tribes and made them part of his dominion.

Some of these conquests had been very recent and were accompanied by forced resettlement of the conquered peoples. Four tribes south of the James River—the Nansemond, Warraskoyack, Quiyoughcohannock, and Weanock—had fallen to Powhatan. In the early 17th century, just before the arrival of the Jamestown colonists, his warriors also virtually exterminated the Chesapeake tribe, which lived at the mouth of what is now called Chesapeake Bay. The action was in response to a prophecy that a nation that would spell doom for Powhatan's chiefdom would arise in the Chesapeake's lands.

The village of Kecoughtan, north of the James River, had been conquered in the 1590s after the death of its chief. Its population was then resettled in other villages, other people were moved onto their former land, and Powhatan's son Pochins was made the werowance over them. Another of Powhatan's sons, Parahunt, now ruled over the original Powhatan tribe. Yet another son, Tatacoope, expected to become chief of the Quiyoughcohannock, because his mother was the weronsqua of that tribe. It is likely that the Paspahegh tribe had also recently suffered Powhatan's onslaught, for their territory was sparsely inhabited when the

Chief Powhatan and lesser werowances stored shell beads such as these in their temple treasuries. The beads served both as ornaments and as currency.

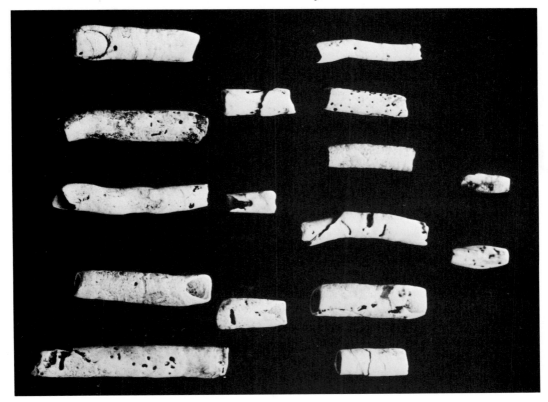

A map of Virginia from Captain John Smith's Generall Historie of Virginia *(1624). At the center is the vast area inhabited by the tribes then under Chief Powhatan's rule.*

English colonists decided to establish Jamestown there. Under the eyes of the English, Powhatan's warriors in 1608 would conquer the Payankatank, who lived on the river known by their name. The former residents of Kecoughtan would then be resettled there.

Powhatan was far more than a werowance. He was the *mamanatowick*, or "great king," over all his tribal chiefs, who were compelled to pay him huge tributes of skins, beads, copper, and foodstuffs. He stored these goods at a safely remote treasure house and temple in the woods near Orapaks, one of his inherited territories. His own residence, however, was at Werowocómoco, meaning "chief's town." There he employed a full-time personal guard of about 50 of the tallest warriors in his dominion. This was the closest thing to a standing army in the area, because men were usually warriors only when not at their daily labors. The principal holder of wealth and power in his dominion, Powhatan also had the largest number of wives of any man therein: About a dozen lived with him at any given time. After a woman had borne him a child, Powhatan would bestow her upon a worthy member of the upper class and might then take another wife in her stead. He had created strategic alliances by marrying some of his daughters to important werowances both within and outside of his realm. Moreover, Powhatan's three brothers, Opichapam, Opechancanough, and Kekataugh, were werowances in the Pamunkey area and potential heirs to their eminent sibling's post.

At the end of the 1500s, the only tribe in the region between the Payankatank and Blackwater rivers that paid no tribute to Powhatan was the Chickahominy. Their domain, which extended along the river bearing their name, was completely surrounded by that of Powhatan. The Algonquian-speaking Chickahominy, one of the largest tribes in the region, called their leaders *munguys*, meaning "great men."

Powhatan's rule also did not extend to the tribes living along (and sharing the names of) the Rappahannock and Potomac rivers, or to the Accomac, across Chesapeake Bay. Trade and alliances created an uneasy peace between these sovereign peoples and the Powhatan tribes. But some of the independent tribes, especially those living along the Rappahannock, probably feared they might become the objects of his next war of conquest, even though most of their villages were safely located on the north side of the river. To the south, the Dismal Swamp and the strong Iroquoian tribes called the Nottoway and Meherrin formed obstacles to further expansion of Powhatan's domain. His people still conducted occasional raids, however, into the Roanoke River valley. By the time the Powhatan tribes first greeted the future settlers of Jamestown, the Indians may have numbered between 15,000 and 20,000—perhaps even more.

Whether the experiences of Don Luis with the Spanish in years past had any historical impact on the rise of Powhatan and his people can only be guessed. But a century of intermittent, mostly hostile contact with Europeans had in some ways prepared this complex society of "savages" for the Englishmen whom they now sat down to entertain and feed. ▲

NOVA BRITANNIA.

OFFERING MOST

Excellent fruites by Planting in
VIRGINIA.

Exciting all such as be well affected
to further the same.

LONDON
Printed for SAMVEL MACHAM, and are to be sold at
his Shop in Pauls Church-yard, at the
Signe of the Bul-head.
1609.

*An illustration from a 1609 British pamphlet seeking recruits for
Virginia, here also referred to as Nova Britannia, or New Britain.
Despite the promise of "most excellent fruites," the first settlers
depended on trade with the Indians for their very survival.*

POWHATAN, POCAHONTAS,
AND
PEACE

The English at Kecoughtan seemed to make friends easily. The villagers offered them seats of mats spread out on the ground, then fed them corn bread. They also proffered a pipe of tobacco, which their visitors smoked without understanding that this act was intended to symbolize the peaceful intentions of both parties. In their own effort to promote feelings of friendship, the English distributed glass beads, pins, needles, and bells. After years of occasional acquaintance with white men, the Indians had in fact come to expect such goods from them.

As the English continued up the James River, they paid calls on various villages. At Paspahegh, the Indians delivered speeches in their own language, which the Englishmen did not understand. The werowance of Quiyoughcohannock received his visitors by playing the flute, another source of puzzlement. At Appamatuck, the chief met them holding forth his bow and arrows in one hand and a tobacco pipe in the other. The prospective settlers interpreted his speech as indicating that he wanted them to leave; in fact he was offering them a choice between war and peace. At each village the English presented the Indians with gifts, which were always accepted. But the gift giving caused envy in those who had been overlooked and also raised an appetite for more.

Bells and a token, excavated from Jamestown. English colonists traded items such as these to the Powhatan people in exchange for food and furs.

The English colonists had come to North America to get their share of the continent's wealth. They could not see why Spain should be the only country to profit from the exploitation of the region and its native inhabitants. Their justification for taking control of the land and resources in Virginia was that no other Christians had settled there; by establishing a colony they might, in the words of the colonial charter, spread Christianity "to such people as yet live in darkness and miserable ignorance of the true knowledge and worship of God." In short, the English argued that they and the Indians were engaged in a deal that was profitable for both peoples: The Indians would give up some of their land to the English and receive Christianity in return. But this proposition was never presented to the Indians for consideration, for the English felt they knew what was best

for the Powhatan peoples and discussing the matter would be absurd.

If the Indians had fully understood the intentions of the English, they would likely never have let them set foot on their land. But they could not know at the outset whether these foreigners proposed simply to fish and hunt there, to trade, or to settle. Powhatan was at first content to keep close watch on the encroachers through his minions. But Sir George Percy would soon note that the Powhatan people "murmured at our planting in the Countrie"—for this indicated a stay of indefinite duration.

By mid-May 1607, the settlers had chosen an unoccupied island in the James River as the site of their first settlement and began to fortify the area. When the werowance of Paspahegh and his warriors paid them a visit, the English suspected he had come to drive them away, but he had in fact brought a fat deer for their dinner and seemed willing to offer them more land to settle. After all, he would surely gain from having direct access to English goods. But one of his warriors did not think it necessary to wait for trade and took a hatchet. The English drew their swords and muskets and recovered the object by force. The werowance then ordered his men to leave before general fighting could begin.

The mixed signals sent by the Indians during events such as this puzzled and disturbed the English and ultimately provoked deep suspicion as to the Indians' motives and intentions. In truth, the Indians shared their mistrust—and rightly so. This mutual apprehension was compounded by the differing cultural outlooks of the two groups. Nor did either party apparently take into account that perhaps the other group held clashing viewpoints among themselves and could not always speak with a single voice.

Later in May, a group of colonists traveled up the James River to investigate the region and its inhabitants. Their new Indian neighbors scrutinized them in turn. On this trip the English first heard of the great king Powhatan, but they met only his son Parahunt at the village of Powhatan, and later one of his brothers, perhaps Opichapam. The settlers were received with kindness wherever they went, but the temptation to steal English possessions proved too great for some of the Indians to overcome. The colonists in turn mis-

led the tribes as to their true intentions. After setting up a cross at the falls of the James River to claim the land for the king of England, they told Parahunt that it signified their firm alliance with him, especially against the Powhatans' Siouan enemies.

Although the trip seemed a success, when the explorers returned to Jamestown they found that an estimated 200 Paspahegh warriors had attacked and almost overrun the fort, perhaps because they were angry that the English had traded with other tribes. The colonists, seemingly unable to distinguish between one tribe and another, found all this very difficult to understand. They did not know whether they should trust or fear the Indians they met. One colonist, Gabriel Archer, wrote of his confusion after returning from the expedition to the falls: "[The Indians] are naturally given to treachery, [yet somehow] we could not find it in our travel up the river, but rather a most kind and loving people."

In June, two of the colonists' ships returned to England under the command of their original captain, Christopher Newport, who promised to return soon with fresh supplies. About the same time, Powhatan sent his first direct message to the inhabitants of Jamestown. He announced his interest in establishing a peaceful and friendly relationship with the settlers and said that he had ordered his people to let the colonists plant and harvest their own crops. Throughout that summer, the Indians brought gifts of food.

But rather than providing for the well-being of the colony, the gentlemen settlers spent much of their time struggling for power among themselves. Their provisions were soon gone. Sir George Percy wrote in his diary that some colonists fell victim to "cruell diseases . . . Swellings, Fluxes [bloody discharges], Burning Fevers, and by warres" and that more "died of meere famine." Illnesses—probably typhoid and dysentery, caught by drinking the brackish river water—ravaged the settlers and kept the men from building houses. Some of the colony's laborers ran away to live with the Indians, who welcomed them because their knowledge and skills could be highly useful. By November 1608, the Jamestown survivors numbered 40 out of an original 100, a terrible loss kept secret for fear of a Powhatan massacre.

Captain John Smith, a member of the colony council, decided to go on trading expeditions in the settlers' remaining ship to procure corn from the Indians' fall harvest. Smith, a renowned adventurer whose reputation had preceded him, was not considered a gentleman by his supposed betters; indeed, he had been imprisoned for a time during the transatlantic voyage, on a trumped-up mutiny charge. But his fortunes had risen even as those of his incompetent associates declined.

At first Smith was successful enough. He was a shrewd bargainer, and his command of the Algonquian languages, although poor, nonetheless outshone that of fellow colonists. But the nearby Indians would not risk starvation just because the whites had been improvident. After nearly depleting the corn supply of neighboring villages, Smith moved on to Chickahominy territory, where the people were eager for a share of English trade goods.

During one of these expeditions, Smith was taken prisoner by a hunting party led by Powhatan's brother Opechancanough, after a brief battle in which several Englishmen and Indians were killed. The hunters took the captain to a site on the Rappahannock River where a European ship had visited a year or so before. The captain of that vessel had killed the local werowance and kidnapped some tribesmen. Smith was tried and cleared of this charge and also passed an examination by the priests, who determined that he was harmless—perhaps meaning that he had no magical powers. Opechancanough himself marveled at Smith's compass, treated him very well, and finally took him to meet the great Powhatan himself.

What exactly happened when Smith and Powhatan met at Werowocómoco will never be known. Smith was the only one to tell the story, and he modified it several times during his lifetime. (Considering the cultural and language barriers, Smith probably hardly understood the encounter.) It seems certain that Smith entertained the mamanatowick with stories about the world across the ocean and then—probably in hopes of saving himself—lied about the reasons the English remained on the Indians' territory. Rather than telling Powhatan that they had come to North America to establish a colony, Smith said that the one remaining English ship had been damaged and that the settlers were now waiting for Captain Newport to return and take them home again. His western explorations on the Chickahominy River, Smith continued, were to find a way to "the backe Sea" (that is, the Pacific) and to reach the other side of the continent, where Powhatan's Siouan enemies had killed an Englishman. The exploration claim may well have been partially true, as the English took every opportunity to investigate the uncharted continent.

What Powhatan thought of Smith's story cannot be known. But Smith's claim that Powhatan then sentenced him to death and that he was saved only by the intervention of the chief's daughter Pocahontas (who was little older than 10 at the time) is probably not true. The ritual Smith perceived as his imminent execution may have actually been a ceremony that would have made Smith an adopted member of Powhatan's tribe. The chief subsequently told Smith that he wanted the

A modern reenactment of the construction of buildings in Jamestown. As the colonists began to plant fields and build houses, the Powhatan realized that their visitors planned to make a permanent new home in the tribes' territory.

captain to live near him, as his subject, at Capahowasick. Powhatan offered to feed Smith and his fellow settlers if they would in turn make him iron hatchets and copper ornaments.

The same evening that Powhatan released Smith, the Englishman returned to Jamestown to find that Captain Newport had arrived with fresh supplies from England. But the entire colony nearly perished in a major fire a few days later, making the settlers dependent once again on the Indians' corn supply. Smith returned to visit Powhatan. He requested the Indian leader's aid and presented him with a white dog, a red coat, and a hat. Smith also

falsely promised to give Powhatan firearms and to join him in raids against his enemies.

Now using the young Pocahontas as his messenger, Powhatan liberally supplied the English with "bread, fish, turkies, squirrels, deare and other wild beasts," Smith later wrote. He even proclaimed Smith a werowance. But the English, for their part, intended the reverse to occur: that Powhatan should become subordinate to the king of England. After Captain Newport returned to Jamestown with supplies in September 1608 following a second voyage, Smith went to Werowocómoco to deliver more gifts, including an English

A narrative engraving from Captain John Smith's Generall Historie of Virginia *showing how, after a brief battle in a Tidewater swamp, the Pamunkey "tooke him prisoner in the ooze." Chief Powhatan soon freed Smith, however, and eventually named him a tribal werowance.*

bed. On this visit, he tried to put a coronet on the head of Powhatan, who—annoyed by a ritual no one had explained to him—refused to kneel or even bend his knees to signal submission to the Crown.

After a short period of contact, both the English and the Indians thought that they had come to dominate the other, but nothing had changed: The English still wanted land, the Powhatan tribes still desired trade, and each distrusted the other for good reason. The English, still short of food, increasingly used force to obtain provisions from Indian stocks. Powhatan in turn began to use the settlers' hunger to extort guns, swords, and other items.

The following year, 1609, was bad for both the colonists and the Indians. Supplies expected from England did not arrive after a hurricane scattered, then wrecked, the fleet in the Bahamas. Nonetheless, the established settlers attempted to start up new communities in Nansemond territory, southeast of Jamestown, and at the falls of the James River. The Indians resented this expansion, and the number of murders committed by both the English and the Indians increased. Because rainfall that summer was sparse, the corn crop fell short of all expectations. Indian villagers, lacking enough to feed even themselves adequately, promptly returned runaway settlers to Jamestown.

In October 1609, John Smith left Virginia. Earlier that year, he had been badly burned when a spark accidentally ignited his powder bag. While he was recovering, he was deposed by his political enemies from the colonial presidency to which he had been elected the previous year. For all his cleverness and force, Smith had been unable to guarantee peace between the Indians and the colony. After his departure, the situation became desperate. The colonists were starving, and the few who lived to see the arrival of supplies, in May 1610, convinced the supply ships' captains to take them home. Jamestown was to be abandoned, and it seemed Powhatan would regain total control of his territory.

But as the colonists prepared to leave Virginia that June, three ships under the command of Thomas West, baron de la Warr, brought reinforcements of more than 300 settlers and plenty of provisions to the colony. With them came a new policy: The Indians would be forced to accept English rule. The colonists destroyed Kecoughtan within a month; Paspahegh, a month later. The settlers of Jamestown had long been intimidated by the non-European methods of warfare employed by the Indians. Accustomed to rows of uniformed soldiers who fought in precisely organized battles, the English had instead encountered guerrilla raids, sneak attacks, and ambushes. Now, in merciless retaliation, they destroyed the Indians' cornfields, ransacked their temples, killed Indian women and children, and set whole villages on fire.

By these steps the English established a strong foothold in Virginia, seizing control of the lower Virginia peninsula from the mouth of James River to Jamestown and establishing themselves at the river's falls as well. Regularly provisioned, they raised their own corn crop and began to keep cattle. Under de la Warr's decisive military leadership, they took the offensive, conquered the villages of the Appamatuck and Arrohateck on the James River, and installed plantations in their place. They remained at peace with the small Quiyoughcohannock and Kiskiack peoples, however, and perhaps even continued to trade with them.

Powhatan was undoubtedly upset by this complete reversal of fortunes. Yet, after seeing some of his tribes destroyed, he may have been afraid to attack the English at full force. His warriors made occasional raids, but these were not enough to dislodge the settlers. The English were now able to replace corn lost in Powhatan forays by trade with the Potomac tribes or with the Accomac on the Eastern Shore across the bay.

While Powhatan brooded over his dilemma, the English scored a major coup. In April 1613, Admiral Samuel Argall was engaged in trade along the Potomac River when he heard that Powhatan's daughter Pocahontas was visiting a local village. By bribing the brother of the Potomac werowance, Argall managed to lure her aboard his ship. He took Pocahontas hostage, aiming to exchange her for English prisoners held by her father. During the negotiations that followed, Pocahontas,

now 18 years old, was brought to Jamestown, where she was detained for almost a full year.

Over that period, Pocahontas began to display an active interest in the English way of life. She allowed herself to be instructed in Christianity and was baptized, becoming the Powhatan tribes' first convert. At her baptismal ceremony, she took the Christian name of Rebecca. On a more worldly plane, Pocahontas fell in love with John Rolfe, a widowed English planter 10 years her senior. (Rolfe was the very man who had introduced Brazilian tobacco to Virginia, giving the colony a major cash crop.) Her affections were returned. But because marriage between an Indian and a colonist was such an extraordinary occurrence, Rolfe sought advice from his mentors. In a letter to the colonial governor, Rolfe wrote,

> I freely subject myselfe to yor grave & mature Judgement. . . . My hart and best thoughts are and have byn a long time soe intangled & inthralled [with Pocahontas]. . . . Lykewyse addinge heereunto her greate appearance of love to me [is] her desyre to be taught and instructed in the knowledge of God, her Capablenes of understanding, her aptnes, and willingnes to recyve any good impression, and also the spiritual besides her owne incytements stirringe me upp hereunto. What shoulde I doe?

The couple married in April 1614. Virginia's colonial leadership readily approved of the match, seeing it as a way by which they might achieve lasting peace with Powhatan. The mamanatowick himself may have been too old and tired to oppose it. He did not attend the wedding, but afterward he kept peace with his daughter's new in-laws and left the routine duties of tribal governance to his brothers.

The end of the hostilities between Powhatan and the Virginians also made the independent Chickahominy tribe open to peace. Shortly after Pocahontas's wedding, the Chickahominy agreed to sign a treaty in which they promised to become Englishmen and subjects of King James I. In exchange for metal hatchets, red coats for their munguys, and some portraits of their new ruler, they pledged an annual tribute of 1,000 bushels of corn. Two years later, however, the Chickahominy refused to pay the tribute, partly because the harvest had been very poor, and perhaps partly because they no longer felt threatened by their neighbors. The English then proceeded to attack them, only to learn that their former allies had

Ætalis suæ 21. Aᵒ. 1616.

Pocahontas, also known as Lady Rebecca. This portrait was painted by an unknown artist in England, perhaps during Pocahontas's visit there in 1616–17.

now found protection under the rule of Powhatan's brother Opechancanough. It did not, in fact, make too much difference to the English, as long as peace was preserved. ▲

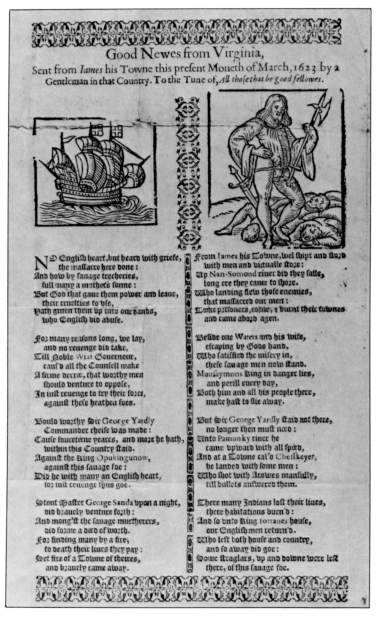

Good Newes from Virginia,

Sent from *Iames* his Towne this prefent Moneth of March, 1623 by a
Gentleman in that Country. To the Tune of, *All thofe that be good fellowes.*

NO Englifh heart, but heard with griefe,
　the maffacre here done:
And how by fauage trecheries,
　full many a mothers fonne:
But God that gaue them power and leaue,
　their cruelties to vfe,
Hath giuen them vp into our hands,
　who Englifh did abufe.

For many reafons long, we lay,
　and no reuenge did take,
Till Noble Wiat Gouernour,
　caufd all the Counfell make
A firme decree, that worthy men
　fhould venture to oppofe,
In iuft reuenge to try their force,
　againft thefe heathen foes.

Bould worthy Sir George Yardly
　Commander cheife was made:
Caufe foureteene yeares, and more he hath,
　within this Country ftaid.
Againft the King Opukingunow,
　againft this fauage foe:
Did he with many an Englifh heart,
　for iuft reuenge thus goe.

Stout Mafter George Sands vpon a night,
　did brauely venture forth:
And mong'ft the fauage murtherers,
　did forne a ded of worth.
For finding many by a fire,
　to death their liues they pay:
Set fire of a Towne of theires,
　and brauely came away.

From Iames his Towne, wel fhipt and ftord
　with men and victualle ftore:
Up Nan-Somond riuer did they faile,
　long ere they came to fhore.
Who landing flew thofe enemies,
　that maffacred our men:
Tooke prifoners, come, & burnt their townes
　and came abord agen.

Befide one Waters and his wife,
　efcaping by Gods hand,
Who fatiffied the mifery in,
　thefe fauage men now ftand.
Monfymons King in danger lies,
　and perill euery day,
Both him and all his people there,
　make haft to flie away.

But Sir George Yardly ftaid not there,
　no longer then muft need:
Unto Pamunky riuer he
　came vpward with all fpeed,
And at a Towne cal'o Cheffkeyer,
　he landed with fome men:
Who fhot with Arowes manfully,
　till bullets anfwered them.

There many Indians loft their liues,
　there habitations burn'd:
And fo vnto King Iottanes houfe,
　our Englifh men return'd.
Who left both houfe and countrey,
　and fo away did goe:
Some ftraglars, vp and downe were left
　there, of this fauage foe.

An English broadside of a ballad titled "Good Newes from Virginia." Printed in March 1623, one year after Powhatan warriors killed more than a quarter of the colony's population in a surprise attack, it celebrates the survivors' fortitude.

OPECHANCANOUGH'S WARS

Powhatan, having reached at least 70 years of age, died of natural causes in April 1618, and his brother Opichapam (also known now by the name-title of Itoyatin) succeeded him as mamanatowick. But this new ruler was rarely seen or heard by the colonists. Another brother, Opechancanough, had long held considerable sway over the tribes, and with Powhatan's death he soon gained effective control of them. Initially, both the figurehead and actual chief publicly supported continued peace with the English colonists.

Although the truce had already lasted four years, the Virginians still kept a watchful eye on their Indian neighbors, who far outnumbered them. In the year of Powhatan's death, Samuel Argall, governor of the Virginia Colony, ordered the settlers not to remove the barriers that protected their plantations. He further warned against private trading with the "perfidious savages" to prevent the Indians from discovering how few people inhabited the settlements. He also wanted to keep Indians from obtaining European firearms, which were considered an especially serious threat to colonial security. Guns had indeed been given to Indians by runaway white servants and sold to them by greedy traders, even though disseminating firearms was illegal.

Opechancanough at first maintained an attitude of cordiality, for a number of reasons. One was that he still coveted English goods such as weapons, wool blankets, copper kettles, iron knives and hatchets, and glass beads. But he did not want other things the English offered him, namely Chris-

47

King James I (1566–1625), who ascended the English throne following the death of Elizabeth I. James actively supported the building of a boarding school for Virginia's Tidewater Indian youths.

tianity and allegiance to King James. Opechancanough found alliance with the colonists desirable only to the extent that it increased his power.

Another reason Opechancanough did not initially resist the colonists was that the Powhatan tribes had been plagued by a series of natural calamities. Epidemics of smallpox, measles, influenza, and other dreadful diseases swept through the entire Indian population of the Tidewater region in 1617 and 1618. These maladies had been brought to North America by Europeans, and because the Indians had never been exposed to the diseases before, they had developed no immunity to them. As a consequence, the Indians were extremely vulnerable to illnesses that were less often fatal to the disease-acclimated English (although smallpox terrified even them).

Pocahontas herself fell victim to some such scourge in March 1617. Powhatan's daughter, now known as Lady Rebecca, had voyaged to England the previous year with John Rolfe and their tiny son, Thomas, accompanied by an Indian entourage. Some European intellectuals of that era idealized Indians as "natural" human beings—people who lived in perfect harmony with nature and were free of the selfishness, aggressiveness, and irrational behavior supposedly bred by a corrupt civilization. Consequently, Pocahontas was lionized by the elite of London society, where the "noble savage" was—at least in the abstract—the latest word in chic. But Pocahontas's health began to decline. The dank English winter apparently took its toll on her, perhaps compounded by London's air pollution and oppressive urban environment. The family prepared to return to Virginia that spring, but Pocahontas grew so ill that she was removed from her ship at the last moment. She died on English soil, having perhaps reached 22 or 23 years of age, and was interred in a chapel in the county of Kent.

In Virginia, the Indian epidemics were aggravated by other problems. The wild deer population was also hard hit by disease, and droughts killed off the corn harvests. These losses so impoverished the tribes that they were unable to pay off their debts and tributes to the colony; indeed, they now found themselves trading with the English for corn. The colony used the opportunity to acquire more land for the cultivation of tobacco, on which Virginia's continued existence had come to depend.

The English project of converting the Powhatan to Christianity made little progress after the conversion of Pocahontas. Some young men and women who had gone to London with her were placed in English homes to be reared as Christians, but often they were simply used as cheap labor. One young Indian man was educated in England by a man named George Thorpe, who would soon play a major role in Virginian affairs. The Indian boy learned to read and write and subsequently became Thorpe's secretary, but he was baptized only days before his death—probably by illness—in 1619. The surviving Indian women of the entourage—still unconverted after five years—were sent in 1621 to Bermuda, another British colony, where they were married off as quickly as possible. They had been, in effect, exiled from their homeland so as to prevent their backsliding into traditional ways.

Englishmen also raised money to build a college—in modern usage, a boarding school—for the education of Indians. King James himself strongly endorsed the project. Its establishment was delayed, however, in large part because the Indians were reluctant to part with their children.

In 1619, Opechancanough proposed, through his ambassador Nenemattanaw, a joint Powhatan-British expedition against the chief's Siouan enemies to the west, to avenge the murder of some Powhatan women. The Virginia Colony's council in London approved the proposal, not so much for their portion of the spoils of war as to oblige the mamanatowick and to obtain as captives Indian children, who could then be placed in the proposed college. Although this proposed expedition fell through, the council also authorized Virginia's governor to give Opechancanough whatever he liked best from the colony's stores.

These attempts to bribe Opechancanough into allowing Indian children to be brought up as Christians were intensified in 1621 with the arrival of a new governor, Sir Francis Wyatt, in Virginia. He was accompanied by George Thorpe, who took the lead in winning over Opechancanough to their cause. Thorpe showered the mamanatowick with gifts, including an English-style house, complete with door and lock, and an illustrated geography book. He also criticized the colonists for their prejudices, saying that the Indians had received "nothing but maledictions and bitter execrations." A little more kindness in dealing with the Indians, he thought, was all that was needed to make them see the light.

But it had become too late for a new and better beginning. Just as many colonists felt the Indians to be the source of all their misfortunes, the Indians had come to realize the English wanted far more than trade and that peaceful co-existence had led only to disease, loss of land, and death. In reaction, a religious movement arose among the Tidewater Indians, proclaiming the superiority of the Indian way of life and promised a return to the days of Powhatan's glory.

Opechancanough's subordinate Nenemattanaw numbered among the leaders of this resistance movement. Sir George Percy noted that Nenemattanaw was known to the colonists as Jack of the Feathers because he had formerly marched into battle against them "all covered with feathers and swans' wings fastened to his shoulders as though he meant to fly." Now he claimed to possess an ointment that made him invulnerable to the bullets of English guns.

Nenemattanaw's boasts reached the colonists, as did rumors of an Indian conspiracy against the English. A religious ritual held in 1621 was said to have been part of a plot to poison the settlers. Opechancanough denied all such insinuations, but Nenemattanaw persisted in provoking the colonists. He soon paid for this dearly. After Nenemattanaw killed an Englishman, he went to his victim's plantation wearing the man's cap. He was apprehended, then shot in an ensuing brawl. His last request was to be buried among the colonists so that none of his countrymen would know he had died by a bullet.

The colonists feared Opechancanough would be enraged by news of Ne-

nemattanaw's death. But he showed no anger and even told the governor "he was contented [Nenemattanaw's] throat was cut." Opechancanough may well have been furious, but he was also clever enough not to want the English to know it at that time. Whatever the reasons, he tried to reassure the governor that "the sky should sooner fall than peace be broken."

Opechancanough also let George Thorpe believe he was about to be won over to the Christian God. Late in 1621 he consented to a new treaty intended to pave the way for the conversion of his people. The mamanatowick insisted that the articles of peace be stamped in brass and hung from an oak tree near his residence. For the next three months, perfect harmony seemed to prevail between the Indians and the newcomers. Unarmed Indians visited the settlements, bringing game, fish, and furs to trade for glass beads, cloth, and tools, and they were always welcomed by their English hosts. This peace turned out to be an illusion.

On the morning of Good Friday, March 22, 1622, Indians came to the plantations to trade and visit, just as they did on any other day. Some had stayed overnight in colonists' homes; others sat down to enjoy breakfast with their hosts. Without warning and acting as one, the Indians grabbed the Virginians' weapons and fell upon them. Before they were driven off at the day's end, some 330 settlers, more than a quarter of the settlement's population, were dead. Among them was George

Thorpe. His body was cruelly mutilated as if to drive home the point that all deals to exchange land for Christianity were off. Among the survivors was Pocahontas's widower, John Rolfe, who died later that year of natural causes.

What the English saw as a massacre, however, the Indians perceived as an act of their new religious faith. Some attributed the act to their god Okewas, who was said to have incited them against their own will. Though Nenemattanaw had died, his beliefs had avenged him.

Opechancanough's attack had caught most settlers by surprise. But it

A 17th-century engraving, by Theodore de Bry, of the Powhatan warriors' slaughter of Virginian colonists on Good Friday, 1622. The settlers retaliated with a campaign to annihilate the tribes.

did not succeed completely because at least two compassionate Indians had disclosed the plot to the English at the last moment. One, the servant of a planter, had visited England before Opechancanough's uprising and would return there in 1624. The other had lived among the colonists, employed as a hunter. He chose to remain among his people, and later became Opechancanough's ambassador to the settlers. The warnings of these two saved many, but colonial settlements were too spread out to alert everyone in time and many colonists were killed.

The slaughter radically transformed the colonists' perspective. They had previously assumed, naively, that the Indians wanted to be converted and "civilized." Now it was clear the Indians had no intention of peacefully allowing their land to be seized by strangers. Opechancanough's war also provided the colonists with the justification to wage an all-out campaign, not merely to dominate but to destroy the enemy tribes. Because the English were now afraid to plant corn, lest the Indians use the cover to sneak up on the survivors, they devoted all their time to war against their Indian neighbors.

In the fall of 1622, after the colonists had received fresh supplies and instructions from England, they began to carry their warfare to more distant locales. The London-based council of the Virginia Company had directed them to

> pursue and follow [the Indians], surprising them in their habitations, intercepting them in their hunting, burning their towns, demolishing their temples, destroying their canoes, plucking up their weirs [dams for catching fish], and carrying away their corn.

By pursuing these tactics, the colonists hoped to clear the country of the Powhatan tribes during the coming winter. And, indeed, by early 1623 they claimed to have killed more Indians over the previous year than in all the earlier years since 1607 combined. Still the war between the colonists and the Indians was far from over.

But not all the Tidewater tribes had been part of Opechancanough's uprising. Some had no part of Powhatan's chiefdom, nor were their territories immediately threatened by the English. Among these were the Potomac and the Accomac of the Eastern Shore. These peoples remained neutral in the conflict and indeed even continued their trade with the English.

Hoping to gain time in which to regroup his starving forces, Opechancanough offered a truce. In a show of good faith, he released one Englishwoman taken prisoner in 1622. She returned dressed "like one of their queens," noted one colonial document—a display intended to show both the Indians' good treatment of English captives and their high regard for their adversaries. The colonists had their own surprise for Opechancanough when they met with him and some of his werowances in May 1623 to ransom the remaining pris-

An image of the god Okewas, in a 1590 engraving by Theodore de Bry. Powhatan warriors commonly carried the idol into battle, and some claimed Okewas inspired the 1622 massacre.

oners. At the end of the peace talks, the English offered their enemies poisoned wine and then fired their guns at the drugged and drunken Indians. As the surprised party fled, Opechancanough was seen to fall, and colonists subsequently sent word to England of his death—reports that turned out to be slightly premature.

More English raids followed, leaving the Pamunkey tribe, of which Opechancanough was werowance, in dire straits. In July 1624, more than 800 war-riors of the Powhatan tribes, united under Opichapam (for his brother may have been in hiding), were forced to defend the vast cornfields they had planted to replenish their empty stores. For two days they fought a pitched bat-tle against the English, who ultimately destroyed the Indians' crops.

The Pamunkey lost not only their food supply but also their reputation among their neighbors as great war-riors. Neutral Indian spectators from as far off as upper Chesapeake Bay had come to observe the widely heralded battle, just as if it were a prize-fight. Moreover, although the English had virtually exhausted their supply of gunpowder in the clash—and thus could not have moved against any other forces—they managed to keep the depletion secret, and frightened tribes began to desert their villages. The English settlers further reinforced their territory by running a barrierlike fence across the narrow neck of land between the James and York rivers.

With the passage of time, the balance of power shifted more and more in favor of the colonists, who possessed superior technology, a growing population, and immunity to the diseases that continued to devastate the Indians. Occasionally the Indians managed to take some settlers prisoner or kill some of their cattle, but on the whole they fought only in defense. In 1628, the English concluded a largely meaningless treaty with Opechancanough in order to retrieve their prisoners of war. But fighting flared up every summer during the corn season until 1632, when the colonists finally made peace (through a treaty now lost) with the Pamunkey and Chickahominy tribes, who had regained some of the independence they

Drawings of the species of tobacco native to North America (left) and native to Brazil (right). Colonist John Rolfe introduced the Brazilian variety to Virginian planters in the early 1600s. The crop rapidly gained great monetary importance to the colony.

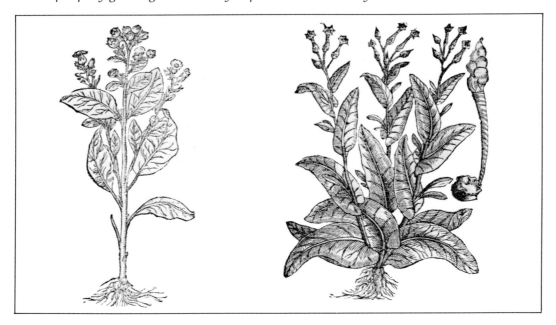

had enjoyed before Powhatan's and Opechancanough's rule.

Under these conditions of almost perpetual warfare, peaceful contact between most Indians and colonists became exceedingly limited. Settlers who dared to meet secretly with any Indian were liable to be punished severely, as colonial authorities hoped to drive the Powhatan tribes to their knees by making it impossible for them to trade for European goods. Only a few traders had licenses permitting them to barter with Indians, and they could deal only with the peaceful tribes along the Rappahannock and Potomac rivers and on the Eastern Shore, across Chesapeake Bay. Selling firearms, of course, was outlawed, but even trading glass bottles and cloth to most Indians was prohibited. The Indians nevertheless desperately requested these and other trade items, which shows the extent to which in a few years they had become dependent on European products.

Ten years of war had been terrible for the Powhatan tribes. But the 12 years of peace following the treaty of 1632 were perhaps even worse. The Indian population continued to decrease steadily, primarily from disease. White planters continued to transform the tribes' ancestral lands into their own tobacco fields. Opechancanough's chiefdom had lost its greatness, and his people had been shaken in their belief in the old ways.

On April 18, 1644, Opechancanough made a last stand. Now at least 80 years old and unable to walk unaided, the mamanatowick once again mounted an offensive to drive the English from Virginia. Possibly Opechancanough initiated this campaign after hearing that a civil war was raging in Great Britain, and anticipating that the colonists themselves had become divided and weakened by the conflict.

But however the English civil war may have affected the colonists, Opechancanough's second uprising never had a hope of success. Colonial Virginia had become so densely populated that even a fairly small band of Powhatan warriors sufficed to kill 400 settlers in the war's opening assault. But there were so many colonists now that this loss had little impact, and once the tribes' advantage of surprise was gone, it took the English only two summers of attacks on Powhatan villages, combined with an unrelenting destruction of their cornfields, to beat the tribes into submission.

Opechancanough remained defiant to the end. When captured in 1646 he refused even to acknowledge his defeat, and was carried to Jamestown and jailed. Curious colonists crowded about his cell to gawk at the architect of two bloody wars and the brave leader of his people. Although the mamanatowick had lost his cause, he never signed a treaty. One of his guards, an English soldier enraged by the number of colonists killed in Opechancanough's wars, shot the imprisoned ruler in the back. ▲

This medal, inscribed to "the Queene of Pamunkey," was given to Cockacoeske by Charles II of England in 1677.

STRANGERS
IN THEIR
OWN LAND

In October 1646, Necotowance, the new mamanatowick of the Powhatan tribes, signed a treaty that formally ended Opechancanough's wars. This treaty, like earlier ones, proclaimed the tribal leader to be a subject of the king of England. But, in distinction to times past, the Indians were now so weak that they had become truly dependent on the colonists, who by this time outnumbered them three to one. The annual tribute of 20 beaver skins Necotowance was required to give the colonial governor under the treaty's provisions was not necessary for the colony's survival, as earlier tributes of corn had been. It was, rather, an acknowledgment of the Indians' subordinate position, tendered in exchange for their protection by the colonial government against undefined "rebels or enemies."

By the treaty's terms, the Powhatan also ceded to the English the land between the James and York rivers all the way to the rising Piedmont slopes—a concession that split their territory in two. Necotowance found it difficult to make his warriors recognize the new boundaries and understand that they could no longer return to their old homes and hunting grounds without running the risk of being shot on sight. Some called him a liar and learned the truth the hard way.

The region north of the York and south of the James was still reserved for the Indians. No colonist was to enter these territories without the Indians' permission, but those planters already settled north of the York were authorized to remain there for three years. At the end of this period, when Necotowance came to pay his tribute in March 1649, he told the governor (according to an anonymous tract published that year) "that the sun and moon should first lose their glorious lights and shining before he or his people should evermore hereafter wrong the English." As proof of his friendship, he gave the colonists permission to pass through his dominion "at all times when and where they please."

Necotowance disappears from all English records after this single pronouncement and may not have lived to see the tide of land-hungry planters that had begun to inundate the country once reserved for his people. With his apparent departure from the scene, most of the Powhatan tribes came to be governed only by their individual werowances; and the Chickahominy were ruled once more by their munguys.

Lacking the sense of unity that had once been championed by a supreme ruler, the fragmented people of the Powhatan tribes grew even more vulnerable to colonial expansion. In October 1649, three werowances petitioned the colonial legislature for grants of 5,000 acres for each of their tribes. And in 1650, the legislature passed a law reserving land for Indian towns, allowing 50 acres per warrior. Similar laws were enacted or amended every couple of years—invariably decreasing the "protected" acreage—as colonists continued to appropriate what little land remained in Indian hands. Werowances filed complaints and petitions with colonial authorities again and again, but some tribes—especially the smaller ones—were quickly pushed from the fertile lands they had cleared along the rivers. Some peoples, such as the Powhatan proper, vanished during this era, while others emerged by splitting off from larger tribes. Tribal reservations diminished throughout the rest of the 17th century, as did the Indian population.

But the treaty of 1646 had also, wisely, regulated contact between the Indians and the colonists; without such restriction, the Indians might well have been killed without exception. The only Indians allowed to enter the colony were messengers sent by the chiefs. To be recognized as such they had to wear striped coats, like prisoners. (Later this provision was modified so that Indian visitors wore copper or silver badges inscribed with the name of their werowance.) Because of this limited communication, few Indians learned to speak English, and most business between Indians and colonists had to be conducted through interpreters.

In 1646, entertaining or concealing Indians within the bounds of English territory—an act considered to be a risk to colonial security—became an offense punishable by death. Yet two years later, when some planters in York County were rumored to be receiving Indian visitors in their houses daily, colonial authorities ordered that only the Indians be killed and that the whites be punished in a less drastic fashion. Soon it was discovered that killings of Indians under this directive were often motivated by "some private malice," and the law was changed the following year to punish only those visiting Indians who actually caused harm.

Indian servants were among the few Powhatan not barred from the colony. Some of these were actually prisoners of war from previous skirmishes with the English, and their status differed little from that of the colony's black slaves. Spanish traders had introduced African slaves to Spain's American holdings possibly as far back as the early 1500s. But English settlers had possessed none until 1619, when a Dutch ship visiting Jamestown sold a cargo of slaves to the community's tobacco planters. That transaction established the institution of slavery in the agricultural colonies, whose slave population would grow rapidly over the coming century, with resounding consequences for both the white and Indian peoples of the Tidewater region.

A clause in the 1646 treaty also allowed Indian children under age 12 to live as voluntary servants with white planters. Some Powhatan parents, mostly among the Accomac tribes of the Eastern Shore, encouraged their children to become servants in colonial homes so that they might learn English and discover how best to deal with whites. Elsewhere in Virginia, however, this practice was quite uncommon. Whites, on the other hand, frequently kidnapped Indian children

In 1646, as colonial governor of Virginia, William Berkeley signed a treaty pledging to defend the Tidewater Indians against "rebels or enemies." Some 30 years later, he himself would be deposed from his position during a settlers' revolt.

for use as servants. If caught, they generally claimed to have purchased them from the child's parents or werowance. Antikidnapping laws were eventually passed to stop this abuse.

Indians did, however, have means other than servitude by which they could earn the money needed to buy English goods. From 1651 onward, colonial authorities allowed settlers to pay Indian hunters to kill wolves, which posed a threat to livestock. (The hunt-

By the mid-1600s, glass beads obtained in trade with the English had largely supplanted the Powhatan's traditional shell beads as jewelry and currency.

ers were not permitted, however, to use firearms, only bows and arrows or traps.) Such employment soon became commonplace, even though the white employers were required to obtain a license and put up a monetary bond for their hunters as security against any havoc they might inflict. Indian women contributed to their household budget by making and selling pots that combined the traditional techniques of working clay with vessel shapes suitable for use by the colonists.

Although Indian access to white settlements remained limited throughout the 17th century, the colonists apparently felt less constrained to keep off Indian property. Servants on the colonial plantations seemed to find Sunday visits to the nearest Indian town a major source of entertainment, "to the great disquiet of the Heathen," as an observer noted in 1662.

When the Indians complained about English encroachment on their lands, the colonists in turn protested the Indian warriors' practice of killing their hogs. Planters commonly let their livestock, which were identified only by a property mark in the animals' ears, freely roam the woods around their property. The Indians, however, disregarded the marks, because they did not share the European concept of animal ownership. When, some time before 1657, a colonist complained about such poaching to a local werowance, the tribal leader apologized but added that colonists had likewise taken some of his deer. The colonists then pointed out that the domesticated pigs were marked, but the deer were not. The werowance retorted, "Indeed, none of my deer are marked, and by that you may know them to be mine; and when you meet with any that are marked you may do with them what you please; for they are none of mine." As European ways became more widespread among the natives, however, they too began to raise hogs, and within 20 years the Indians themselves were marking their livestock.

Although the Powhatan tribes had become subordinate to the colony, individual Indians were nonetheless treated as foreigners, not as British citizens. They paid no taxes because they were still to some extent self-governed. Colonial authorities interfered in the tribes' internal affairs only to the extent that new werowances had to be confirmed by the governor. Crimes committed between Indians were settled among themselves.

But whenever there was a dispute between the Indians and the English, a double standard became apparent. If, for example, an Indian killed or even threatened to kill a colonist, he was sure to be hanged. And until the culprit was apprehended, all the people of the nearest Indian village were held responsible for the crime. The white murderer of an Indian, however, was usually punished according to the tribes' traditional system of justice, in which the culprit atoned for the crime by the payment of shell beads to the victim's survivors.

Despite the avowals of years past, the settlers now made little effort to convert or "civilize" the Indians—that is, to introduce European ways and fashion them into mock Englishmen. The disillusionment produced by the colonial massacre of 1622 was too deep-seated for this notion to take root again. One such project, which subsequently failed, aimed to give Indian hunters a cow for every eight wolf heads they delivered to colonial authorities. The colonists thought that if the Indians owned cattle they would become "civilized" because this would give them, according to the law itself, "something to hazard and lose besides their lives." The incentive of private property, however, failed to raise the warriors' interest in wolf hunting. They preferred to take payment for such work in barter, to use as they saw fit.

Yet Powhatan's descendants were not wholly indifferent to European ways. Some native people left their tribes, managed to purchase their own land, and became English citizens. Ned Gunstocker, a Nansatico Indian from the Rappahannock River region, even joined the English militia to fight "my countrymen, the Indians." Most, however, remained in their own communities and adapted to English culture (a process known as *assimilation*) only to the extent that it seemed to benefit them.

The Powhatan tribes continued to raise corn, beans, squash, and other native plants. Some planted apple orchards, but native tobacco had been almost totally supplanted by the colonists' imported Brazilian variety. Fishing and gathering mussels and wild plant foods remained important means of obtaining food, and county courts usually granted permits allowing Indians to leave their reservations for these purposes. The little land the Indians still retained hardly sufficed as hunting grounds, yet hunting remained the major contribution of Indian men to the larder. After 1658, colonial authorities, feeling that the danger of war was past, even permitted the Indians to use guns on their reservations. Some tribes began to raise hogs, and a few wealthy individuals also owned horses.

Most Indians continued to live in their traditional mat-covered dwellings. A few werowances could afford wood-frame houses or were given them by colonists. By now cloth and glass beads were commonly used to make clothing and ornaments. Cloth, like shell beads, had become a currency that could readily be exchanged for English money.

Traditional beliefs and practices endured, in part because of the lack of Christian missions among the Powhatan. Priests kept the temple fires burning and recorded tribal history in pictures painted on deerskins. They also continued to perform rain-bringing ceremonies, sometimes even for neighboring white planters, who nonetheless believed the priests to be in league with the devil. As in the past, some young people braved the ordeal of the coming-of-age ritual known as the Huskenaw.

Although Powhatan's confederacy of tribes had collapsed, individual werowances remained powerful. One such leader was the weronsqua Cockacoeske, known to the colonists as the Queen of Pamunkey. She had inherited her position by her relation to the late mamanatowick Opechancanough, but the colonial government mistakenly regarded her husband Totopotamoi as the Pamunkey tribe's true leader. Totopotamoi achieved literary fame when he was mentioned in a comic verse epic, *Hudibras*, by the 17th-century English poet Samuel Butler:

This precious Brother having slain,
In times of Peace, an Indian,
(Not out of Malice, but mere Zeal
Because he was an Infidel)
The mighty Tottipottymoy

Sent to our elders an envoy,
Complaining sorely of the Breach
Of league, held forth by Brother
    Patch.

Although in the mid-17th century warfare no longer held the importance it once had in Powhatan society, it had not disappeared. The once-victorious tribes now defended their territory to the north against a number of tribes, including the Iroquoian tribes known as the Five Nations, and against the Tuscarora to the south. In 1656, English militiamen asked help from both the Pamunkey and Chickahominy against other Indians marauding the frontier. The tribes gladly accepted the challenge, but through the incompetence of the English commander, the detachment was defeated and Totopotamoi killed.

The last major military confrontation between colonists and the Indians of the Tidewater region came in 1676, with an episode known as Bacon's Rebellion. At the time, high taxes, low tobacco prices, and a severe drought had already caused the colonists great hardships. The threat of Indian attack was the only spark needed for these tensions to ignite into violence. The previous year, colonial militiamen had mistaken a group of friendly Susquehannock Indians for hostile warriors and attacked them. The Susquehannock had revenged themselves by raiding plantations along the frontier. When the colonial government raised taxes yet again to pay for increased se-

NATHANIEL BACON THE
YOVNGER, CALLED
The Rebel
BORN JANV-
ARY 2ᵈ 1647
DIED OCTO-
BER 1ˢᵗ 1676

Nathaniel Bacon, the leader of Bacon's Rebellion in 1676, as depicted in a stained-glass window from Bacon's Castle in Surry County, Virginia.

curity, a young planter named Nathaniel Bacon, Jr., united the disgruntled colonists.

The insurrectionists found it easier to make war on the neighboring Indians than to attack the root causes of discontent. Making war on the most visible tribe, the Pamunkey, was also a way of vicariously attacking the colonial governor, Sir William Berkeley, the same official who had promised the Indians protection against "rebels or enemies" under the treaty of 1646. The rebels also claimed that Berkeley had monopolized the Indian trade for his own benefit, when in fact the licensing of traders was to protect the Indians against fraud. Finally, they argued that the Indians should be punished for causing the crop-killing drought with their sorceries.

Bacon's forces so intimidated the Pamunkey people that they deserted their village and hid in a nearby swamp. The rebels then turned against the Susquehannocks, who had fortified themselves near the Siouan tribe known as the Occaneechi. Bacon managed to persuade the Occaneechi into routing the Susquehannock from the settlement for him, but then Bacon's men turned on the Occaneechi and killed most of them.

After managing to depose Governor Berkeley, Bacon once more turned his attention to the Pamunkey people in the fall of 1676. The Indians put up no resistance when Bacon at last located their camp in the swamp. The Pamunkey were shot or taken prisoner. The rebel leader then paraded the captive survivors around Jamestown to demonstrate that he was indeed an honorable Indian fighter. After Bacon died of natural causes a few weeks later, his rebellion collapsed. But popular sentiment remained against those Indians still in captivity. Some colonists suggested unsuccessfully that they be sold into slavery—even though the Indians had been the victims rather than the perpetrators of the crimes.

In May 1677, a new treaty was concluded between the colony of Virginia and the Pamunkey, Weanock, Appamatuck, and Nansemond tribes. The document reaffirmed the tribes' status as subjects of the English Crown, added a symbolic payment of 3 arrows to the annual tribute of 20 beaver skins, and

The opening and signature pages of the published peace treaty of 1677 between Charles II of England and the leaders of several Tidewater tribes. Among the signers were the rulers of the Pamunkey, Nottoway, Nansemond, and Roanoke peoples.

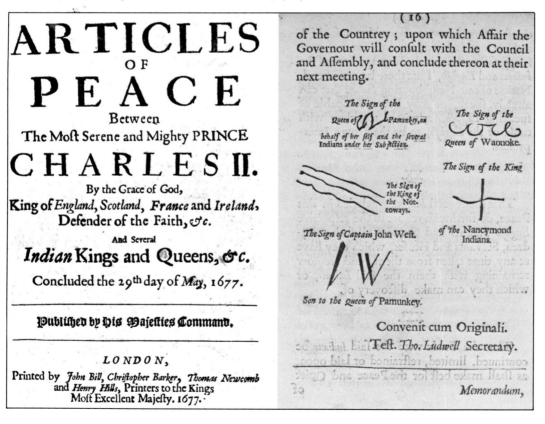

reinstated Cockacoeske, the Queen of Pamunkey, as ruler over "several scattered Indians" who "now again own their ancient subjection." This last clause asserted Cockacoeske's power over the Chickahominy, who promptly notified the authorities they had no intention of relinquishing their independence.

Under the treaty the colony established a new reservation for each tribe, each area protected by a three-mile buffer zone not to be settled by neighboring whites. But their territory shrank as tribes fled the confinement of their crowded villages for land still unsettled by anyone. Some smaller groups merged to form new tribes. Yet, at the same time, quarrels and rivalries led to discord and even violence among the people of those villages.

Many such disputes sprang from the clashing viewpoints of Indian traditionalists with those who supported assimilation into the colonial culture— either because they considered that culture superior or because they simply felt assimilation was inevitable or prudent. The products of colonial culture were indeed not only everywhere around them but were now more easily attained than ever before. All trade restrictions had been removed shortly after Bacon's Rebellion. Indians were even permitted to own guns. Except for pottery and basketry, most traditional crafts—such as carving, hide tanning, and ornamental work—were slowly falling into disuse as native goods were replaced by English equivalents. Only children now used bows and arrows, so men, no longer worried about entangling their locks in the weapons, began to wear their hair long on both sides. People continued to observe traditional religious practices and to speak their native language, yet even some Indian priests acknowledged that their magic had been unable to depose the Bible or anything English.

Alcohol became universally available, its popularity enhanced by the illusion of freedom that drunkenness briefly gives. It became pitifully common to see Indians staggering drunkenly down the streets of colonial Jamestown and Williamsburg, yelling and cursing, because they thought this would finally make them like Englishmen. ▲

Brafferton Hall, on the campus of the College of William and Mary, in Williamsburg, Virginia. Brafferton was originally built to house Tidewater Indian students at a boarding school established at the college in 1723.

MATTERS OF RED, WHITE, AND BLACK

By the end of the 17th century, fewer than a thousand Indians remained in all of Tidewater Virginia—about 1 percent of a total colonial population of 100,000. Their numbers would continue to shrink drastically over the next hundred years, but for different reasons than before. Since the Indians first came in contact with Europeans, epidemic disease had been the leading cause of death among the Powhatan. Wars and other forms of violence had taken their toll as well. But by 1700, the Indians had developed immunities to the diseases the colonists had introduced, and Virginia's Indian wars were over. Now the Powhatan tribes' most dangerous enemy was colonial society itself—its prejudices, its discriminatory laws, and

its fears, all of which brought discord and division into the very fabric of the Indian communities.

The dramatic decline in the number of Indians in Virginia's Tidewater region had coincided roughly with the dawn of black slavery in the South. While the region's Indian population dwindled even more over the course of the 1700s, its slave population grew in tandem with the plantation system, as white tobacco planters thrived. As a result, colonial Virginia became, like the cotton-based Deep South, an essentially biracial culture, divided into free whites and enslaved blacks. Many southern whites in fact did not own slaves, and some southern blacks were free men and women. Nonetheless, the institution of slavery—with its relent-less emphasis on race—came to affect deeply the values and attitudes of all southerners. Its effects extended even to the remnant Indian population, which was forced to operate within the framework established by the dominant culture.

These cultural strictures led to the passage of a series of laws, known collectively as a "black code," enacted by Virginia's colonial assembly in 1705. Before that time, the rights of the Indian population had been officially defined largely by treaties between the colony and the land's native population. Now domination was so complete that the colony no longer sought the consent of the tribal werowances before changing its rules for coexistence.

The new laws did reaffirm the special status of reservation Indians. They prohibited anyone, including Indians, from trying to sell off the Indians' remaining communal lands without governmental consent. The laws also protected the Indians' traditional right to gather wild plant foods "and other things, not useful to the English," even outside the reservations and prohibited the sale of hard liquor in Indian villages. They even gave the reservation Indians the same legal protection afforded colonists.

At the same time, however, the black code classified those Indians living outside the reservations as "free persons of color," a legal status they shared with free blacks and mulattoes

(people of mixed black and white ancestry). Indians so classified were now prohibited from hunting on lands claimed by white Virginians. They were also barred from holding public office and from serving as witnesses in courts of law. Marriages between Indians and whites had already been outlawed in 1691, despite the example of Pocahontas and John Rolfe. Now children with one Indian parent were defined as mulattoes, whether the other parent was black or white. Moreover, all children were classified as mulattoes if they had one black parent, grandparent, or great-grandparent. Only a thin line—a bloodline—now separated a reservation Indian, who possessed acknowledged rights and privileges, from an off-reservation one, who was legally designated as "colored" and had a much lower social status. Although the latter were not enslaved, some plantation owners probably forced their Indian servants into marriage with blacks, so that the children could be claimed as slaves.

One reason the laws of 1705 were passed was the murder of a white family by Nansatico Indians the previous year. This tiny tribe, living in northern Virginia, had experienced problems with encroaching white neighbors and had asked colonial authorities for a just settlement. When no help was forthcoming, some Nansatico warriors put on war paint and took their own vengeance, killing the family of John Rowley, one of the white intruders.

Consequently, the entire tribe—comprising 49 men, women, and children—was apprehended and jailed. Five Nansatico men were tried, convicted of the murders, and hanged. Although authorities found the remaining 44 not guilty, the adults were subsequently deported to the West Indies, the children were pressed into servitude to white planters until they reached adulthood, and the tribe's homeland was sold off. For their warriors' crimes, the Nansatico people had been wiped from the map.

The end came for other tribes of Tidewater Virginia in a less dramatic fashion. The Weanock and Appamatuck, in Southside Virginia, had been gradually pushed off their reservations before 1705. The Appamatuck continued to live on the plantation of William Byrd, an English trader for whom some tribe members worked. Over time they merged with the neighboring black population. The Weanock chose to join their old enemies, the Iroquoian-speaking Nottoway, finding that they shared more with these traditional adversaries than with the white colonists. A few members of the Nansemond tribe also developed ties with the Nottoway while persevering on an ever-shrinking reservation; the last five residents sold their plot with permission of the colonial assembly in 1792 and gradually assimilated. Still another group of Nansemond had in years past intermarried with whites but, because of their long residence and good reputation in the

William Byrd, a Virginia planter, who harbored most of the members of the Appamatuck tribe on his vast plantation. Byrd wrote in his diary: "All nations of men have the same natural dignity. . . . The principal difference between one people and another proceeds only from the different opportunities of improvement."

area, they were able to maintain their status as an officially recognized tribe without living on a reservation.

North of the York River, the Chickahominy tribe, although numbering around 16 families in 1722, lost its reservation sometime in the 1720s as the result of internal strife; some wished to

Thomas Jefferson, third president of the United States, in an engraving made after a portrait by De Quevanillier. Jefferson's observations on various Tidewater tribes made up part of his Notes on the State of Virginia.

assimilate, while others wanted to maintain their traditional culture. Some Chickahominy remained near their old lands, but others probably drifted south. In the eyes of the law, they ceased to be Indians. The same was true of the remnants of the Rappahannock and Potopaco tribes, who lived scattered and without recognition among their white and black neighbors. By 1705, the Wicocomoco of the Northern

Neck had also been reduced to a handful of people; but Robert Beverley, a historian of the period, noted that "[they] keep up their kingdom, and retain their fashion." After the death of their last werowance in 1718, however, this tribe disintegrated as well. By the end of the 1700s, only the Pamunkey Indians and the Accomac of the Eastern Shore had managed to maintain their reservations and rights as recognized Indians.

Through several land sales, by 1748 even the Pamunkey reservation, located in King William County, was split into 2 parcels 10 miles apart on the Pamunkey and Mattaponi rivers. To protect this land, the Virginia colonial assembly in 1748 appointed three white trustees from the vicinity of the reservation (the number was later increased to six, all serving lifetime terms of office). Later, these trustees would come to advise Pamunkey leaders on other matters as well, such as the settlement of internal disputes.

By 1759, Indiantown—as the Pamunkey reservation was commonly known—was said to be home to "the few remaining of that large tribe, the rest having dwindled away through intemperance and disease." Andrew Burneby, a visitor, noted that "they commonly dress like the Virginians, and I have sometimes mistaken them for the lower sort of that people." Alcohol abuse had certainly hastened the Pamunkey's decline, but their seemingly imminent disappearance resulted, in fact, largely from cultural assimilation.

On or off the reservation, most Indians now lived in log houses, wore European-style clothes, and had adopted English-style names. Many were discernible only by their skin color, which was usually dark enough to be judged "nonwhite." Those able to pass as white usually did so, because in the face of discrimination and prejudice there was little reason to want to be regarded as Indian.

Only as most of Powhatan's tribes were vanishing did the colonists begin to offer Indians an English education. In 1723, colonial authorities erected an Indian school, as part of the College of William and Mary in Williamsburg, Virginia, to instruct all Indian youths who could be coaxed into attending it. Because there were usually not enough Indian pupils, vacancies were often filled by English youngsters. In 1723, Brafferton Hall was built to house the Indian students.

For the next 50 years, a number of Pamunkey youths (probably all young men) received instruction in reading and writing (in English), arithmetic, and Christianity. In the school's early years, it was said by Hugh Jones, a clergyman, that many of those Pamunkey who returned to the reservation reverted to "their own savage customs and heathenish rites." Nevertheless, these students greatly influenced the already changing ways of Indiantown. By 1800, virtually all the Indians of the Tidewater had become Christians. However, the turmoil of the American Revolution (1776–83)—in which the British colonies won their independence and Virginia thus became a state—resulted in an end to money for Indian education.

In 1787, Thomas Jefferson—a William and Mary dropout who later became the third president of the United States—described the remnants of the Powhatan tribes thus:

> There remain of the Mattaponies three or four men only, and they have more negro than Indian blood in them. They have lost their language. . . . The Pamunkies are reduced to about 10 or 12 men, tolerably pure from mixture with other colors. The older ones among them preserve their language in a small degree, which are the last vestiges on earth, as far as we know, of the Powhatan language.

Jefferson's remarks on the extinction of the Powhatan languages—taken from a book about his home state titled *Notes on the State of Virginia*—were lamentably accurate; when, in 1844, a short vocabulary was collected from two old Pamunkey ladies, only the word they used for "one" was found to be a genuine Powhatan word. The rest of the vocabulary was derived from a rhyming game. Only a few isolated Powhatan words remained in use among Tidewater groups by the early 1800s, and even these would be lost by around 1900.

Jefferson's assertion that "negro blood" had eclipsed the Mattaponi's Indian lineage, however, was probably

The capture of Nat Turner, leader of a slave rebellion in southeastern Virginia in 1831, as portrayed in a 19th-century engraving. The bloody uprising led to harsh legal constraints on "free persons of color," a legal category that was considered to include nonreservation Indians.

based on hearsay. Although some Powhatan people had intermarried with blacks or whites, most had wed within their tribes. This is indicated by the fairly small number of Powhatan family names.

In 1831, the Indians of Tidewater Virginia—both those on reservations and the free persons of color—were badly jolted by the repercussions of a nearby slave revolt, known as Nat Turner's Rebellion. In August of that year, Turner, a deeply religious slave called The Prophet by fellow blacks, led an insurrection in southeastern Virginia's Southampton County. Nearly 100 slaves joined Turner, and they killed about 60 white men, women, and children before militiamen and troops crushed the uprising.

By November 1831, Turner and several of his associates had been hanged, but the incident resulted in a backlash that was swift, harsh, and far reaching. New laws clamped down tightly not only on slaves but on free negroes and mulattoes as well. Tidewater Indians now found it crucial to legally prove their ancestry, as best they could, to avoid falling under the new edicts. This was a burdensome task, given that many were barely literate and that state archives of marriage and births were chaotic at best. Such a muddle could only encourage unsubstantiated claims that the Powhatan people had undergone irreversible "racial dilution."

In 1845, for example, a historian wrote of the Pamunkey, "Their Indian character is nearly extinct, by intermixing with the whites and negroes." Ten years later, an anonymous visitor claimed Indiantown to be inhabited "by the most curious intermixture of every color and class of people."

These rumors were probably actively promoted by the Pamunkey's white neighbors, because the charge provided a good excuse to take control of the Indians' land. In 1843, a number of citizens of King William County submitted a petition to Virginia's state as-sembly claiming that the inhabitants of Indiantown "would be deemed and taken to be free mulattoes, in any Court of Justice; as it is believed they all have one fourth or more of negro blood." As such, the entreaty concluded, the community's residents had no right to live there and should be removed and their reservation sold without delay. The assembly rejected this petition, however—at least partly because a second petition by the Pamunkey begged for pity, stating, "There are many here who are more than half blooded Indians, tho we regret to say that there are some [Indians living] here that are not of our tribe."

In fact, the neighbors' charges were not wholly unjustified, for when the two parcels of the Pamunkey reservation had become almost depopulated through slow attrition, the survivors had sought desperately to reverse the trend. Among those recruited to this end were some whites and a number of off-reservation Indians whose ancestry the state government no longer recognized. By 1840, some Catawba Indians from South Carolina had also joined the Pamunkey. Most of the new inhabitants were indeed either Indian or white, but not all were so classified under the law.

As the Civil War approached, the Pamunkey had very nearly seen their reservation abolished because of Virginia's hurtful laws against blacks and mulattoes. The experience taught them, out of sheer self-preservation, to avoid those groups and to appear as recognizably "Indian" as they could. ▲

George Major Cook, chief of the Pamunkey Indians (1885–1930) in a photograph taken in 1918 by anthropologist Frank Speck. By the end of the 19th century, many Indian men had begun to wear their hair long as a visible sign of their ethnic identity.

SEPARATION
AND
SURVIVAL

Nations frequently name their battleships for illustrious historical figures who, being long dead and buried, have little say over how their names are used. At the outbreak of the Civil War in April 1861, one of the Union's most powerful warships was called the USS *Powhatan*. Considering the status of Virginia's Tidewater Indians, this christening was an ambiguous honor at best. For Powhatan's descendants were now commonly regarded as if they too had in effect disappeared from the face of the earth.

But Virginia's Indian people had actually vanished only in the eyes of whites. Although the Powhatan's language was no longer spoken, it had given the English tongue such words as *moccasin*, *tomahawk*, *raccoon*, and *opos-*sum. Few sitting at the dinner table knew it, but succotash, hominy, and corn bread had first been Indian foods. And many of the cities, counties, and rivers of Virginia bore names bestowed on them by the Powhatan people.

The Indians themselves, however, now commonly wore clothes of homespun cotton, much like those of their black and poor white neighbors. They also shared the churches and family names of these groups. Indeed, state tax rolls no longer even admitted the existence of any Indian people. Those living on reservations were not taxed and therefore did not appear in the official records. Those with their own property were classified not as Indians, but as free persons of color, or, more rarely, as whites.

An early 20th-century Pamunkey trapper with an otter skin. The Powhatan continued to trap otter, mink, and other animals and trade their pelts even after hunting for food had grown less important to the tribes.

Increased assimilation during this period in fact had made the Indian population even less discernible to their non-Indian neighbors than in years past. This was especially true of Indians living off reservation—primarily south of the Rappahannock River, along the Chickahominy, and south of the James. Little by little, whites had pushed the Indian settlements away from the riverbanks and onto the hilly lands in between. As a result, the Indians' economy and way of life had undergone some major changes.

Men continued their traditional tasks of hunting and fishing. They set traps for rabbit, otter, mink, and various birds; and they probably used the skins in trade. Some Indian bands still staged communal hunts in the fall, now using dogs to drive rabbits from the underbrush, then killing them with "throwing sticks," small, clublike hunting weapons. Guns were still scarce except among the reservation-based Pamunkey, because of Nat Turner's Rebellion of 1831. Just as a century earlier colonists had feared guns in the hands of Indians, so now planters feared to allow them into the hands of free persons of color—now mainly blacks and mulattoes. To offset this shortage, the Indian hunters began to use crossbows adapted from European models, as well as bows and arrows.

But hunting became less important to the Indians as more of the wilderness was settled. Men therefore began to take an increasing interest in agriculture. They planted corn, beans, gourds, and some tobacco, much as they had in the old days, but now they buried dead fish in the fields as fertilizer, because arable land was in short supply. Wheat and cotton were also grown now, but the hoe remained, for traditional reasons, the major agricultural implement preferred over the plow. The Indians also had yet to raise domesticated farm animals successfully. They allowed their hogs to run free in the woods and fed the animals only on occasion before they killed them in the fall. Plank boats gradually replaced dugout canoes. Log cabins and shingle-roofed plank houses gave way to wood-frame homes. The advent of railroads also made mass-produced goods more easily available to Indians in rural areas. By the end of the 19th century, even the pots the Pamunkey made by hand for sale could not compete in the marketplace with commercially produced wares.

Just as the Tidewater Indians were surrounded on all sides by white culture, so they found themselves living virtually at the heart of the carnage when the Civil War erupted in April 1861. Virginia was permanently divided by the war. The state joined the Confederacy that same month, but West Virginia split off in turn, becoming a new Union state in 1863. The war's first great battle was fought at Bull Run in July 1861, and several of the bloodiest clashes of the next four years took place in Virginia as well, including Chancellorsville, Fredericksburg, and Spotsylvania. And when the rebel army's

A traditional Mattaponi dugout canoe (left) and a plank boat, which became the Powhatan's preferred mode of water transportation in the late 1800s.

Virginia-born commander, Robert E. Lee, finally surrendered, on April 9, 1865, he did so at Appomattox Court House—named after the defunct Tidewater tribe called the Appamatuck.

The surviving Powhatan people did their best to keep a low profile during the war. They had little motivation to fight when both sides regarded them as marginal citizens at best. Some Chickahominy men served the Union cause, but others left Virginia entirely and eventually came to live with the Ojibwa Indians of Canada until hostilities ceased.

And indeed little did improve for the Indians with the war's end. The Thirteenth Amendment to the U.S. Constitution officially abolished slavery in 1865, and over the next five years the Fourteenth and Fifteenth Amendments were also adopted, declaring that "all persons born . . . in the United States" were entitled to "equal protection of laws," and that their right to vote should not be denied "on account of race, color, or previous condition of servitude." Newly liberated blacks grasped these opportunities of the Reconstruction period and established

Two Rappahannock Indians outside their home, in a 1919 photograph by Frank Speck.

themselves as the social equals of Indians in the rural neighborhoods. But many Indians and whites alike, especially in the towns, regarded free blacks as a threat to their old social and economic status. In response there gradually developed a policy known as *segregation*. This program claimed that people of different races ought to maintain—to quote the 1896 Supreme Court case *Plessy v. Ferguson*—"separate but equal" facilities, such as housing, schools, and transportation. But the new practice, which allowed whites to continue their political dominance over blacks, also adversely affected Indians, whose very existence was frequently forgotten in the prevailing biracial model of society.

In their own communities and on a personal level, most Tidewater Indians continued to be accepted by their white neighbors simply out of long-standing acquaintance. Indian communities also reacted informally to the changing social atmosphere by forming their own churches. By now solidly Christian, the Pamunkey established their own center of worship, the Pamunkey Indian Baptist Church, in King William County in 1865. By 1901, the nonreservation Chickahominy had their own church, the Samaria Indian Baptist Church, and in 1932 the Mattaponi would form their own church too. These voluntarily separate churches reinforced the Indians' sense of their ancestral integrity and gave a moral center to their social life as well.

But whenever nonreservation Indians dared to venture beyond their neighborhoods, they now suffered an ever-present fear of being treated as "colored." For example, if an Indian took a train to Richmond, he or she could expect to undergo the indignity of not being allowed to sit in railroad cars reserved for white use. (Reservation-based Indians could legally ride with the whites, however.)

Such social slights provided strong incentive for non-reservation Indian groups to seek official recognition by the outside world. But how they could do so when they had become so assimilated remained a problem. Men gradually began to demonstrate their "Indianness" by letting their straight black hair grow to shoulder length. In more concerted efforts to make their communities distinctively Indian once again, tribal leaders made intermarriage with non-Indians increasingly difficult. Indeed, the first of the Pamunkey tribal laws, which were published in 1894, stated flatly: "No Member of the . . . Tribe shall intermarry with anny Nation except White or Indians under penalty of forfeiting their rights in Town [that is, on the reservation]."

Pamunkey leaders also began to seek out members of various western tribes who might resettle among and intermarry with the Virginian groups. In 1893, the Pamunkey went to the world's fair in Chicago to promote this plan. Carrying certificates from the governor of Virginia "that they were genuine Indians and had a secure tenure of their lands," according to a newspaper account, they talked with other visiting Indian delegations. Later the Pamunkey even published notices in newspapers as far away as present-day Oklahoma to solicit such fellow Indian homesteaders. But nothing appears to have come from these efforts, or from a more specific plan, noted in another newspaper report in 1894, "to induce immigration from the Cherokees of North Carolina." The Cherokee apparently found little reason to abandon their home for an eastern group popularly rumored to be "colored."

In another effort to gain recognition of their Indian identity, the Tidewater people also began to play to the often naive and simplistic expectations of their white neighbors about "savage" life and behavior. Sometimes this meant wearing feather bonnets, beating tomtoms, and doing "primitive" dances—considerable feats for these churchgoing Baptists, whose ancestors had after all first adapted to European ways simply to survive.

One weapon in their fight for recognition was the legend of Pocahontas. Many white Virginians of the 1800s claimed to be able to trace their descent to Thomas Rolfe, Pocahontas's son. These men and women—many of high social standing—now proudly acknowledged having the blood of American Indian royalty running (though of course much diluted) through their veins. Yet a good number of these very same people looked down on Virginia's

real Indians as "colored." In the same manner, white students residing at William and Mary's Brafferton Hall, which was no longer part of an Indian school, sometimes dressed up in their crude conception of Indian dress to display "dormitory spirit." They even elected officers called great werowance, werowance, quiyoughcosuck, and cronockoe (councillor), reviving for their own juvenile use the great tribal titles first recorded by John Smith.

About 1880, the Pamunkey began to perform a stage version of the story of Pocahontas and John Smith, primarily for white audiences. The tale had already served as the basis of many popular American dramas of the 19th century, and the Pamunkey's own interpretation undoubtedly aimed to remind white Virginians of the debt they owed Pocahontas—and the Powhatan people—for saving Jamestown. And it carried the message that Powhatan's other children were still alive and proud of their heritage.

Just as the Pamunkey play had been inspired by popular drama, so had the costumes. Even if anyone had known exactly how the Pamunkey's 17th-century ancestors had dressed, such scant clothing could never have been worn in the late 1800s, either onstage or off, given the era's straitlaced tastes. Instead, the actors and actresses donned heavily fringed and partly beaded regalia, which grew ever more elaborate with each passing year. Of the other stage props used, the Pamunkey bows and arrows did in fact represent a gen-

(continued on page 89)

PAMUNKEY POTTERY OLD AND NEW

For at least 200 years, members of the Pamunkey tribe—most commonly the women—have been known for their pottery, handcrafted from clay dug from Lay Landing, a site on their reservation.

In the early 1800s, the Pamunkey routinely made dishes, pots, jars, and pipes both for themselves and for sale to non-Indians. Potters strengthened the raw clay by mixing it with pulverized and burned shells from freshwater mussels. They then shaped the mixture by hand into a vessel, smoothed its surface with a mussel shell, and perhaps burnished it with a rubbing stone. Sometimes they might etch an abstract pattern into the object before placing the finished work into a fire to harden.

In the mid-19th century, railroads began to bring cheap, mass-produced kitchenwares into eastern Virginia, and the demand for the Pamunkey's handmade pottery soon decreased. The craft was nearly extinct when the Great Depression indirectly led to its revival. In 1932, Virginia state official D. N. Van Ot, on a visit to the Pamunkey, suggested that they try to sell pottery to tourists to supplement their meager income. At Van Ot's urging, the state set up an on-reservation pottery school, run by a non-Indian teacher. The school's first instructor, William Ross, respected his students' traditions but also introduced them to the use of paint, glaze, the potter's wheel, molds, and the baking kiln.

In recent years, however, some potters have revived the older methods. Today many tribal artisans follow both the ancient and modern ways.

A clay pipe bowl, about 4¼ inches high. This object and those on the next two pages were acquired in 1892–93 from Pamunkey chief Terrill Bradby by ethnologist J. G. Pollard.

A handcrafted cup with 3 legs, measuring 5 inches high and 2½ inches in diameter.

A pipe bowl, about two inches high. The multiple stems allowed five people to smoke it at once.

A two-inch-high pipe bowl. The Pamunkey may have learned to make multi-stemmed pipe bowls from their Catawba Indian neighbors.

A painted oval jar, 5¼ inches high. This and the other objects on these two pages were probably made by students at the Pamunkey pottery school in the 1930s and 1940s.

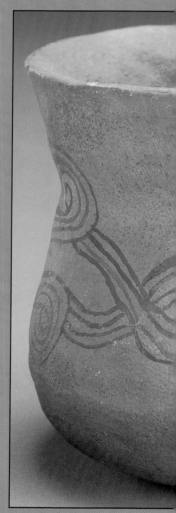

This Pamunkey jar, painted with a delicate swirling pattern, measures only 3¾ inches high.

A jar, 4½ inches high. The Pamunkey used cords, reeds, pointed sticks, or their fingernails to carve designs into wet clay.

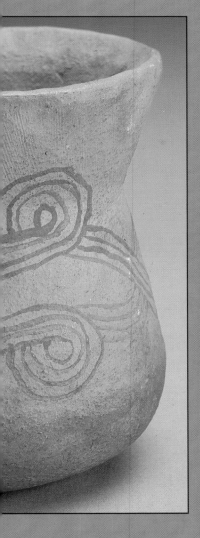

A crosshatch design has been etched into this 3¾-inch jar.

A heavily glazed bowl, about 4½ inches in diameter and painted with white, green, purple, and black pigments. This object and the other two shown here were probably made in the mid-20th century. All are characteristic of the pottery school tradition.

A bowl, 4½ inches in diameter. The designs may have been inspired by those on southwestern tribes' pottery.

A painted 3½-inch vase. Teachers at the pottery school introduced the Pamunkey to pan-Indian designs—patterns used not only by their tribe but by Indians across the country.

A fish-shaped dish, eight inches long and six inches wide, made in the
1930s. Aquatic motifs were popular with Pamunkey potters throughout the
20th century.

A contemporary photograph of the Samaria Indian Baptist Church, near Providence Forge, Virginia. The church was founded by the Chickahominy in 1901.

(*continued from page 80*)

uine survival from the distant past, and the stone axes the actors held had been re-created from prehistoric axheads found in Virginian fields. The "friendship pipes" used in the dramas consisted of four wooden stems inserted into a single clay bowl and had been first introduced to the Powhatan people by the Catawba Indians of South Carolina about 1800. A printed handbill of the period also shows that other acts came to be added, including an appearance by an actor portraying Tecumseh, a Shawnee Indian leader who

was a hero to many American Indians in the early 19th century.

The Pamunkey performed this show for more than 30 years, mostly at places close to home, such as Yorktown and Jamestown, or on the reservation itself in connection with a Forefathers' Festival. But they failed to find financial support to take the play to Omaha, Nebraska, and Paris, France.

How much influence this play had in breaking down the prejudices of the Pamunkey's white neighbors is difficult to tell. In any case, it was for the Indians themselves a very important manifestation of who they were and who they wanted to be. Similar spectacles were later performed on different occasions. The stage costumes sometimes were worn at these and other tribal events, such as the annual tribute to the governor. And Indian parents began to name their children after characters in the play, such as Pocahontas, Powhatan, Opechancanough, Tecumseh, and Deerfoot. This was the first time such names had been used in more than a century.

As the 19th century came to an end, the continued vitality of Virginia's Indian population was at last noted by visiting *anthropologists*—scientists interested in the origins, societies, and histories of all humans. The work of such respected white scholars may have helped offset the prejudices of non-Indian Virginians toward the Tidewater Indians. When James Mooney, an anthropologist working for the Bureau of American Ethnology, visited the Tidewater region in 1899, he wrote to his superiors: "I was surprised to find them so *Indian*, the Indian blood probably being nearly 3/4. . . . Some would pass unquestioned in any Western tribe."

At the beginning of the 20th century, of all the Powhatan tribes only the Pamunkey people still had the reservation land they held since the days of Opechancanough. They continued to give an annual tribute of a deer to the governor of Virginia, and they had their

An 1881 photograph of Pamunkey Indians dressed in the costumes they wore in one of the tribe's stage plays about the story of Pocahontas and John Smith.

own public school. Their relatives on the Mattaponi River had become separated from the main tribal body after the original Pamunkey reservation had been split in half during the 18th century. Now calling themselves the Mattaponi, these people first began to elect their own leaders, and in 1894 the split was officially recognized by the state of Virginia. This group began to pay its own tribute to the governor but continued for some decades to share the church and school of their fellow Indians 10 miles away.

A third tribe of Virginia Indians organized in 1901. This group comprised nonreservation Indians—those people who no longer had any special rights based on colonial treaties. They had come to call themselves "citizen Indians," out of their pride in being voting, taxpaying, and private property-holding subjects. Upon organizing they called themselves Chickahominy, after the river near which most lived. Some possibly were in fact descendants of the old Chickahominy tribe (whose last reservation had actually been on the Mattaponi River); others were Pamunkey who had moved off-reservation, perhaps as far back as the 1640s. This group was not granted a reservation by the state, although it voluntarily delivered an annual tribute to the governor for a while. In 1925, some of them would split off into a separate Eastern Chickahominy group, following religious and social disputes within their movement.

A second burst of renewed Indian consciousness took place during the

A handbill touting an 1898 Pamunkey stage show. Such reenactments proclaimed to non-Indians the Pamunkey's unique ethnic identity.

1920s, due in part to the influence of Frank Speck, an anthropologist at the University of Pennsylvania. Speck had taken a special interest in Indian groups surviving in the eastern United States and began to visit those of Virginia shortly after World War I. His publications, and those of his students, have helped to record some of the traditional lore of these peoples. But his interest clearly went beyond scholarship, and

Chickahominy leaders pay their tribe's annual tribute to the governor of Virginia in 1919.

Speck helped his Tidewater Indian friends in many ways. The various non-reservation Indian communities needed encouragement badly to pursue the task of reorganizing themselves. Some felt intimidated by their non-Indian neighbors and might not have taken such a step on their own. Speck also stimulated contact among the various groups. At one time he even hoped to reestablish a "Powhatan confederacy," but the reservation-based tribes considered a close association with their

"citizen Indian" neighbors to be too socially risky at the time because of segregation laws. Occasionally Speck supplied his friends with Indian-made objects from other parts of the country to remind them of both their own heritage and their kinship with other Indian Americans.

One nonreservation Indian group influenced by Speck had survived near the defunct Chickahominy reservation on the Mattaponi River. In 1919, they were granted a public school of their own, and in 1923, with Speck's help, they organized as a tribe, adopting the name Upper Mattaponi. Two years earlier, their neighbors to the north had incorporated—again with Speck's support—as the Rappahannock tribe. Both groups organized themselves and adopted charters and bylaws under the Virginia State Corporation Commission as Indian associations. The Nansemond also established a loose and short-lived organization in 1923.

Not only did Speck aid all these groups, he stood by them when once again they came dangerously close to having their Indian status denied by law. In 1924, the same year that American Indians across the country were finally given American citizenship, the state of Virginia passed the Racial Integrity Law. Virginia's changing statutes were being used primarily to maintain white social control over blacks, injuring Indians only incidentally. This new law defined whites as people with "no trace whatever of any blood other than Caucasian." However, there was one exception: Individuals who were less than one-sixteenth American Indian were considered white. This saved the descendants of Pocahontas the embarrassment of being denied the right to use the public facilities provided for whites only.

For people not living on a reservation to be recognized as Indians, it was necessary for them to prove that they had no trace of "any Negro blood" and were at least one-fourth American Indian. Reservation Indians qualified as

such only if they had "less than one-sixteenth of Negro blood." In order to establish one's "authenticity" as an Indian according to the law, it became in effect necessary to provide records documenting Indian ancestry for several generations. The apathy, ignorance, and chaotic documentation regarding Indian ancestry outside the reservations in the past—compounded by the wholesale destruction of many Virginia records during the Civil War—produced insurmountable difficulties for many Tidewater Indians in proving their heritage.

Strict enforcement of the law by racist bureaucrats caused untold hardships for Powhatan's descendants. Those who insisted on having "Indian" noted on their children's birth certificates were accused of falsifying the records. Others were ejected from schools and hospitals reserved for whites. Dr. Walter Plecker, head of Virginia's Vital Statistics Bureau until 1946, used his position to denounce people he called "mongrels," who, he claimed, wanted only to achieve "racial deterioration" by marrying with whites.

When the United States entered World War II in 1941, a heated conflict erupted between Indians and the draft boards over the classification of the men inducted. Reservation Indians were inducted as Indians and served in white army units, whereas nonreservation Indian soldiers were classified as blacks. Some were able to get their status changed, but others, especially the Rappahannock, were not, despite the support given by Frank Speck and a few white Virginian friends. Some Indian men were even sentenced to prison terms for refusing to be inducted as blacks. All these trials and sufferings, however, could not break the determination of the Indians to be accepted for who they were. Some left Virginia to find work in the Northeast, where there was less institutionalized discrimination and where their ancestry would be accepted without question, but the vast majority stayed.

During these difficult years, members of several Virginia tribes performed a pageant called "Landing of the English and Their Reception by the Indians." Each May 23rd, the anniversary of the day when the Jamestown colonists first erected the cross at the falls of the James River, the Pamunkey, Mattaponi, and Chickahominy reenacted what the *Richmond Times* called "the initial diplomatic conference between the two races on this continent." After the pageant, the principal of a local school (which Indians were not allowed to attend) delivered an address on "The Day We Celebrate," and Powhatan's descendants performed a snake dance. At the end of the program, the Indian participants always expressed their hope that—in the words of one journalistic account—"the friendly relations existing between the survivors of their once great nation and their paleface brothers will be cherished until the end of time."

After World War II, the prospects of these Indians gradually took an upturn.

The state slowly began to recognize its citizen Indians, to correct their racial classification, and to end their harassment under the Racial Integrity Law as the Vital Statistics Bureau slowly collapsed after Plecker's retirement. Their schools also improved. Virginia Indians had fought long and hard for separate schools, of which they were very proud. However, because the population of the Virginia Indian community numbered less than 1,000 by 1950, these institutions were few, and the scope of the instruction they offered was narrow. On the reservations, the state itself was responsible for public education. Its only effort to teach reservation children about their traditional culture was the establishment of a pottery school on the Pamunkey reservation in 1932. There a white teacher taught students to make pottery using a potter's wheel rather than by the Indians' traditional techniques. He also instructed them to decorate their work with designs he considered to be Indian but that in fact had nothing to do with their heritage. The county governments, which were responsible for nonreservation students, took less interest in specifically Indian-oriented education. At the end of World War II, it was sadly true that, in the words of one state education official, "higher education is made possible for every nationality in Virginia except the Indian."

None of these schools offered instruction above the seventh-grade level, so students had to leave Virginia if they wanted a high school or college

A classroom in the pottery school established on the Pamunkey reservation by the Virginia state government in 1932.

education. Some went to Bacone College, a Baptist school for Indians in Oklahoma. Others were admitted to federal boarding schools for Indians. After 1950, however, a high school was at last added to the Chickahominy's Samaria Indian School, when the tribe raised $800 to buy the land on which the county erected the new school building. Many of the teachers there had grown up in the area and had grad-

uated from Bacone. The Chickahominy could indeed take pride in their hard-won educational achievements. After the school at Pamunkey closed because of its small enrollment (it had only five students in 1948), the state enlarged and upgraded the reservation school at Mattaponi. It produced many fine students. But the Tidewater Indians' pride in their own separate schools would not last forever. ▲

William Miles, a Pamunkey tribe member, on the tribal reservation in King William County, Virginia, in 1989. Behind him stands a memorial to Pocahontas.

LIVING
IN A
DIFFERENT WORLD

For a people who in effect had been given up for dead long ago, the Powhatan tribes were doing remarkably well in the 1960s. Not since the 17th century had there been so many Indians in the Tidewater region—perhaps 1,500 or more. And not for the last 250 years had they had so much pride in being Indian. Many of the old ways were lost, but the peoples' spirit remained.

This resurgence of Indian pride was not limited to Virginia. All over the country, Native Americans rediscovered their rich and diverse heritage. Individual Indian groups also discovered that other tribes across the country shared many of their problems. In order to be better heard, many joined together to form national organizations to

fight for federal, state, and local legislations to achieve their shared goals.

Virginia's Indian tribes differed from the majority of Native American groups enough to join this process only slowly. Unlike tribes that had had a long history of treaty negotiations with the United States, none of the Tidewater groups had ever had any dealings with the government officials in Washington, D.C. Their hold on the land had been broken even before the American Revolution and the establishment of the federal government.

The Pamunkey and Mattaponi, who were recognized by the state of Virginia, had little reason to want to develop a relationship with officials in the nation's capital. At least once a year, when paying their tribute at the state

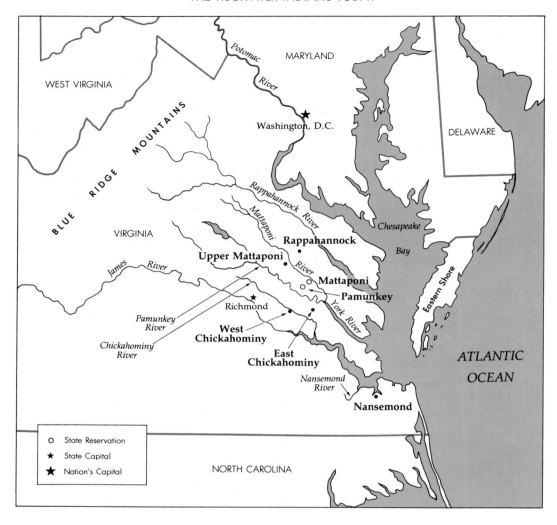

capitol in Richmond, they had direct access to the governor, who alone had responsibility for the administration of Virginia's Indian affairs. The members of these tribes felt lucky to avoid the vast, complicated, and sometimes heavy-handed bureaucracy that they knew federally recognized tribes had to deal with.

Nonreservation citizen Indians, who were recognized by neither Washington nor Richmond, were more eager to band together with other Indian groups. In 1951, the Chickahominy began to sponsor their annual Fall Festival, modeled partly after western Indian powwows and partly on the old local pageants. In the 1960s, they also started to participate in similar events held by other Indians tribes of the East Coast. The Chickahominy who had been to Bacone College in Oklahoma had come into contact with members of many other tribes. Some had even married old classmates, leading to intertribal bonds. Several representatives of the nonreservation tribes of Virginia, such as the Chickahominy and Rappahannock, were present at a 1961 meeting sponsored by the University of Chicago that sparked the modern Indian rights movement by its unprecedented consolidation of native groups from across the country.

Virginia Indians were much less involved in another important social struggle of the same period, the civil rights movement. As part of this movement, blacks and members of other minority groups across the United States called for the end of racial discrimination in schools, the government, and the workplace. Although their goals were similar to those of the Tidewater tribes, the Indians' past experience taught them that a close link with their black neighbors could hurt their own struggle for recognition as Indians.

The civil rights movement had been kindled in part by the 1954 U.S. Supreme Court decision in *Brown v. Board of Education*, which declared an end to racial segregation in public schools. As a result of this ruling, schools were to become desegregated, meaning that students of all races were to be allowed

Chickahominy women performing a dance at the tribe's annual Fall Festival in 1972.

to attend the same institutions. When school desegregation gradually came to pass in Virginia during the 1960s, it became clear that the Powhatan tribes stood to lose the institutions that were the most visible evidence of their heritage—their schools. The smaller schools of the Rappahannock and Upper Mattaponi peoples, along with the reservation school at Mattaponi, were all closed—primarily because of their small enrollments—leaving Samaria school of the Western Chickahominy the only school attended predominantly by Indians in the Tidewater area. When it was fully integrated in 1971, the older generation of Indians—who had bought the land on which it stood and deeded it to the county in order to have an Indian school—went into deep shock.

During this period, the local government also went through a great change. In the past, only whites had been elected to positions of power in county governments in rural Virginia. In Charles City County, for instance, whites—who composed just 9 percent

Members of the Mattaponi tribe marching in a funeral procession following the death of Chief Jacob Vincent Custalow, also known as Thundercloud, in 1982. In the foreground are his brothers Ted Custalow (left, with drum) and Webster Custalow, the succeeding Mattaponi chief (right), along with Rappahannock chief Captain Nelson (center).

Chief Emeritus Oliver "Lone Eagle" Adkins (left), of the Chickahominy tribe, delivers the Lord's Prayer in sign language while Nokomis Lemons of the Rappahannock tribe sings the words. The event was part of the first state-sponsored Native American Indian Day celebration, held in Richmond, Virginia, in 1987.

of the county's population—had always run unopposed by blacks and Chickahominy Indians, who made up 79 and 12 percent of the constituency, respectively. However, the civil rights movement paved the way for the election of blacks as local officials in the early 1970s. Some older Indians worried that their concerns would be pushed aside by these new leaders, just as they had been by the white officials before them. But to their surprise, a Chickahominy was hired as county administrator by a county board of supervisors dominated by blacks; two Indians sat with two whites and seven blacks on the county planning commission; and one Chickahominy joined two blacks on the county school board. The prejudices that had built up over centuries did not immediately disappear, but they became much less pervasive more quickly than anyone could have imagined. The civil rights movement had proved to be beneficial for Virginia Indians as well as blacks.

A Tidewater Indian youth celebrates his cultural heritage with a dance, performed in traditional garb.

Powhatan's people also soon found new ways to convince their neighbors of their Indian ancestry. By participating in national Indian organizations, many had acquired practical information about how to deal successfully with government bureaucrats. In 1971, most of the Indian groups of Tidewater Virginia—reservation based or not—joined with other eastern tribes to form the Coalition of Eastern Native Americans. (The only exceptions were the Nansemond and the Upper Mattaponi.) Membership in the coalition helped Virginia's Indian people gain access to federal funds. Tribes at last became entitled to monies for education, the creation of new jobs, housing improvements, and other programs without having to dig through inaccurate official records to find proof of their Indian ancestry.

Even for the reservation-based Pamunkey, the Indian rights movement and the development of Indian legal defense organizations brought unexpected benefits. In 1971, with the help of the Native American Rights Fund, the tribe initiated a lawsuit against the Southern Railway Company. More than a century earlier, in 1855, the railroad had taken approximately 20 acres of Pamunkey land it needed to run a track to Richmond, without bothering to consult the tribe. The legal battle to regain this land ended when the Pamunkey accepted an out-of-court settlement of $100,000 and the return of 7 unused acres. In doing so, the tribe succeeded in reversing the seemingly inevitable process of Indian land loss in Virginia.

The best evidence of the improved lot of the Powhatan tribes in the 20th century, however, came in January 1983, when the state of Virginia formally recognized the Eastern and Western Chickahominy, the Upper Mattaponi, and the Rappahannock tribes, and established a state council on Indians. (Yet another Rappahannock group and the reorganized Nansemond people would be recognized in 1985.) This recognition was an event for which the Chickahominy had waited almost 83 years to the day. Back in January 1900, the Chickahominy had first petitioned the Virginia state legislature for recognition. At the dawn of the century, few took the request seriously. By the 1980s, many non-Indians remained skeptical, but were now willing to learn. One of these reformed skeptics, a state senator named Wiley F. Mitchell, who served in the state legislature's Indian subcommittee, stated clearly the reason for his new frame of mind: "I found a group of people who have an enormous pride in their heritage and go to great lengths to preserve their ethnic roots."

Given this truth, there is no end to the story of the Powhatan tribes of Virginia. From long before the days of the Jamestown colonists to the closing years of the 20th century, time has not stood still for the Chickahominy and Powhatan's true heirs. Their culture has changed greatly, but so has that of the white people who came to live among them in 1607. But time and bitter struggles have always reminded the Powhatan people of who they are, and they are unlikely to forget it. ▲

BIBLIOGRAPHY

Barbour, Philip L. *Pocahontas and Her World*. Boston: Houghton Mifflin, 1969.

Fausz, J. Frederick. "Opechancanough: Indian Resistance Leader." In *Struggle and Survival in Colonial America*, edited by David G. Sweet and Gary B. Nash. Berkeley: University of California Press, 1981.

Feest, Christian F. "Virginia Algonquians." In *Handbook of North American Indians*, edited by Bruce Trigger. Vol. 15, *Northeast*. Washington, DC: Smithsonian Institution, 1978.

Rountree, Helen C. "Ethnicity Among the 'Citizen' Indians of Tidewater Virginia, 1800–1930." In *Strategies for Survival: American Indians in the Eastern United States*, edited by Frank W. Porter III. New York: Greenwood Press, 1986.

———. *The Powhatan Indians of Virginia Through Four Centuries*. Norman: University of Oklahoma Press, 1989.

Speck, Frank G. "Chapters on the Ethnology of the Powhatan Tribes of Virginia." *Museum of the American Indian, Heye Foundation, Indian Notes and Monographs* 1 (5). New York: Museum of the American Indian, 1928.

Stern, Theodore. "Chickahominy: The Changing Culture of a Virginia Indian Community." *Proceedings of the American Philosophical Society* 96 (April 1952): 157–225.

Vaughan, Alden T. " 'Expulsion of the Savages': English Policy and the Virginia Massacre of 1622." *William and Mary Quarterly, Third Series,* 35 (January 1978): 57–84.

THE POWHATAN TRIBES AT A GLANCE

MAJOR TRIBES   *Chickahominy, Mattaponi, Nansemond, Pamunkey, Rappahannock*

CULTURE AREA   *Middle Atlantic*

GEOGRAPHY   *Virginia coastal plain*

LINGUISTIC FAMILY   *Algonquian*

CURRENT POPULATION   *2,000*

FIRST CONTACT   *Spanish ca. 1525*

FEDERAL STATUS   *nonrecognized*

GLOSSARY

Algonquian A group of languages, spoken by Indian peoples of northeastern America, the Great Lakes, and the Plains, that have similar grammatical and pronunciation patterns and related vocabulary. Algonquian-speaking peoples include the Powhatan tribes, the Narragansett, the Abenaki, and the Cheyenne.

Algonkians The Indian people living in the northeastern United States and east-central Canada who speak Algonquian languages and share numerous other cultural characteristics.

assimilation The conversion or incorporation of a dominated culture into that of the dominant culture.

breechcloth A strip of animal skin or cloth that is drawn between the legs and hung over a belt tied around the waist.

Bureau of Indian Affairs (BIA) A U.S. government agency now within the Department of the Interior. Originally intended to manage trade and other relations with Indians, the BIA now seeks to develop and implement programs that encourage Indians to manage their own affairs and to improve their educational opportunities and general social and economic well-being.

"citizen Indians" A name that a group of Powhatan Indians informally called themselves after 1901, when they officially organized as the Chickahominy tribe. The Indians used the name to indicate their status as voting, taxpaying, and private-property-holding residents of the state of Virginia.

culture The learned behavior of humans; nonbiological, socially taught activities; the way of life of a group of people.

dugout canoe A water craft made by hollowing out the trunk of a tree and treating it with oil or resin to make it waterproof.

Huskenaw The Powhatan ritual by which a select group of boys from a tribe were initiated into its priesthood. See *quiyoughcosuck*.

Jesuit A member of the Society of Jesus, a Roman Catholic order founded by Saint Ignatius Loyola in 1534. The Jesuits are highly learned and, in the 17th century, were particularly active in spreading Christianity outside Europe.

mamanatowick The Powhatan word for "great king." The ruler Powhatan was considered a *mamanatowick* and, in this capacity, received huge payments of tribute from the tribes under his control.

matrilineal, matrilineality A principle of descent by which kinship is traced through the female ancestors.

mission A religious center founded by advocates of a particular denomination who are trying to convert nonbelievers to their faith.

munguy The name that the Chickahominy Indians (one of the largest tribes of the Tidewater region) called their leaders. The word means "great man."

name-title A special term given to a particularly valorous Powhatan tribe member. A name-title could be conferred only by a leader.

Okewas The principal god of the Powhatan peoples. Okewas embodied the spirits of vengeance and terror and, therefore, images of the god were carried by the Powhatan's warriors during wars with rival Indian tribes.

Powhatan Leader of a small Middle Atlantic tribe; in the early 17th century, Powhatan had become the ruler of several neighboring tribes, including the Orapak, the Mattaponi, and the Pamunkey. Powhatan formed them into a confederacy that came to control most of what is now the Tidewater region of Virginia.

quiyoughcosuck The priests of the Powhatan tribes. These men performed rituals and guarded the leader's treasury and the preserved corpses of deceased leaders. They also assisted the tribal leader in seeking out and punishing criminals. See *werowance*.

reservation, reserve A tract of land retained by Indians for their own occupation and use. *Reservation* is used to describe such lands in the United States and *reserve* is used in Canada.

segregation The concept of separating people into mutually exclusive classes based on racial characteristics. Segregation, officially recognized in the 1896 U.S. Supreme Court case of *Plessy v. Ferguson*, theoretically provided minorities (such as blacks and Indians) with "separate but equal" provisions for everyday life. In reality, however, conditions in minority housing, schools, and workplaces were often far inferior to those in white society.

Tidewater region The area of coastal lowlands along the Chesapeake Bay and the Atlantic Ocean in what are now the states of Maryland and Virginia. Before the arrival of Europeans in the 16th century, the Tidewater region was inhabited by the Powhatan tribes and other Indian societies, such as the Tuscarora, Saponi, and Occaneechi.

tobacco A plant native to North and South America that is cultivated for its broad leaves. The dried leaves, which are a mild stimulant, are ground up and ingested either by chewing or smoking.

treaty A contract negotiated between representatives of the United States government or another national government and one or more Indian tribes. Treaties deal with the cessation of military action, the surrender of political independence, the establishment of boundaries, the terms of land sales, and other related matters.

tribe A society consisting of several or many separate communities united by kinship, culture, and language and other social institutions including clans, religious organizations, and warrior societies.

weir A wooden fence or rock wall constructed in a stream to trap fish or force them into a narrow channel where they can easily be netted.

werowance The name used by the Powhatan tribes for a male leader. The position was hereditary and fulfilled both religious and civil leadership functions. A female leader, less common in Powhatan society, was known as a *weronsqua*.

INDEX

PICTURE CREDITS

Ashmolean Museum, Oxford, cover, page 28; The Bettman Archive, pages 12, 36; College of William and Mary Archives, page 66 (photo by Thomas L. Williams); The Daily Press, Inc., Newport News, pages 99, 100; Dementi Studio, page 95 (photo by Christian F. Feest); The Denver Art Museum, pages 84, 85, 88; Department of Anthropology, Smithsonian Institution, pages 81 (cat. # 167520), 82 (cat. # 165453), 83 (left, cat. # 167521); right, cat. # 16545), 86 (left, cat. # 409819; right, cat. # 409820), 87 (cat. # 409821); Courtesy of Christian F. Feest, pages 53, 89, 91; The Thomas Gilcrease Institute of American History and Art, page 46; Jamestown-Yorktown Foundation, pages 19, 23, 41, 60; Library of Congress, pages 16, 18, 20, 24, 27, 29, 30, 31, 42, 45, 48, 51, 55, 69, 70, 72; The Museum of the American Indian/Heye Foundation, pages 33, 77 (photo by M. R. Harrington); National Park Service, Colonial National Historic Park, page 38; The New York Public Library, Rare Books and Manuscripts Division, pages 34, 64; Richmond Newspapers, Inc., page 101; Smithsonian Institution, page 92; Frank Speck, courtesy of the Museum of the American Indian/Heye Foundation, pages 15, 74, 76, 78; George Tames/*New York Times* Pictures, page 96; Valentine Museum, Cook Collection, page 90; Virginia Department of Transportation, page 102; Virginia State Library, page 59; Katherine Wetzel, courtesy of the Association for the Preservation of Virginia Antiquities, page 56, 63.

Maps (pages 2, 98) by Gary Tong

CHRISTIAN F. FEEST is a teacher of anthropology at the University of Vienna. He holds a Ph.D. in anthropology from that university and was a post-doctoral fellow of the Smithsonian Institution in Washington, D.C., and a Ford Foundation fellow at the Newberry Library in Chicago, Illinois. His research primarily focuses on the ethnohistory of northeastern North America, American Indian art and material culture, and European resources for the study of the American Indian. He is the author and editor of more than 100 articles and 6 books, including *Native Arts of North America* and *Indians and Europe*. Dr. Feest is also the curator of the North and Middle American Indian Collections at the Museum für Völkerkunde (Ethnographic Museum) in Vienna, Austria.

FRANK W. PORTER III, general editor of INDIANS OF NORTH AMERICA, is director of the Chelsea House Foundation for American Indian Studies. He holds a B.A., M.A., and Ph.D. from the University of Maryland. He has done extensive research concerning the Indians of Maryland and Delaware and is the author of numerous articles on their history, archaeology, geography, and ethnography. He was formerly director of the Maryland Commission on Indian Affairs and American Indian Research and Resource Institute, Gettysburg, Pennsylvania, and he has received grants from the Delaware Humanities Forum, the Maryland Committee for the Humanities, the Ford Foundation, and the National Endowment for the Humanities, among others. Dr. Porter is the author of *The Bureau of Indian Affairs* in the Chelsea House KNOW YOUR GOVERNMENT series.